Invisible Burqa

BARBARA DOUGLASS

Order this book online at www.trafford.com
or email orders@trafford.com

Most Trafford titles are also available at major online book retailers.

Printed in the United States of America.

ISBN: 978-1-4907-3806-2 (sc)
ISBN: 978-1-4907-3808-6 (hc)
ISBN: 978-1-4907-3807-9 (e)

Library of Congress Control Number: 2014909887

Trafford rev. 05/31/2014

www.trafford.com
North America & international
toll-free: 1 888 232 4444 (USA & Canada)
fax: 812 355 4082

I wish to thank my relatives and friends who helped and encouraged me in this endeavour. I mention especially those people who allowed me to use their stories anonymously. They are: Al, Bob, Chris, Emilie, Grace, Gayle, Haytham, Irena, Larry, Laura, Lilian, Lucy, Marg, Margareth, Mavis, Norma, Renata, and Ruth.

Foreword

I was considering the ideas expressed in this book, and discussing them with my friend, Mary, long before the thoughts ever hit a piece of paper. Much of what we had been taught as children seemed so illogical. The more we read, the more we questioned, "Did God really want us to listen to all these man-made rules? Did we have to eat fish every Friday?" That idea was the least of my personal queries. I really couldn't understand why my friends, who followed the dictates of the other prophets, should be converted by me to follow my particular religious beliefs. In the church I attended, I was told that that was my duty. Many of these friends also did acknowledge Jesus as one of their own prophets. Hence, much reading, and many discussions, I formulated my personal beliefs.

First, I talked with those who attended a place of worship regularly. Most of their reasoning paralleled mine. These people like their place of worship and are accustomed to the regular rituals. Do we all believe that we will die and go to hell if we don't attend regularly? No. Is our attendance just "heaven's insurance" policy since we are mainly either grey, or bald? Well, maybe it is. Some of my friends who don't go anywhere believe that there is absolutely nothing after death anyway. Thus, they think you should just do the best you can while here on earth. Most of these people live exemplary lives. Then, there is this friend who totally renounced the church—did what he believed was right most of the time, and when he had a near-death experience, saw the "pearly gates." So who knows? When you finish, maybe you will understand my beliefs. If you wish to talk to me, which is the purpose of my writing, my ideas can be controversial. Is it time, considering the state of our world, for more such discussions?

The answers from friends who have left a church, or who have never attended one, were different. Almost to a person, they said that they are sure there is a God. They do not believe that He requires them to follow all the manmade rules of any church. Most also believe in and practice the behaviours which Jesus taught, allowing them to have better lives. I think, in particular, of one man who will spend his life helping and loving his friends. He has built many of the places in which we work and live. What a significant contribution! He always does what he believes is right, even when it is at a cost to himself.

Some people go through their lives never questioning their pursuit of illusive goals, goals in which they may doubt and regret in the end. How many material possessions does one really need for security? How will that "security" help you when you are dying? What if you are leaving with real second thoughts about what you've left undone? What if there is no loving person at your side to hold your hand? It is not the number of mourners, which you need or the people who wish that their love would accompany you on your last journey?

I've chosen to write under the pseudonym of one of my former students uses for me: Mom1—in computer language that apparently means I am 'adopted" as his second mother. Some members of my immediate family do disagree with the ideas I am expressing in this writing. Thus, my identity will be hidden, except to those friends to whom I give copies of the book. Two of these people have helped a great deal by using their superior editing skills . . . "I can't believe I'm correcting my English teacher's mistakes!"

Introduction

As a Canadian, I trust I am reasonably similar to most other people who have lived all their lives in Canada. We welcome newcomers to our beautiful and democratic country. We do our best to assure them that they are in the right place, and that we believe they will be happy, and prosperous here. I have helped in the process of these people's learning of English; in so doing, I myself have learned a great deal. I've learned of their challenging pasts, and their hopes for a better future here, especially for their children.

Some of us, however, are having an emotional problem with the desire of those women of certain sects of the Muslim faith who wish to hide behind a burqa. I can understand the use of hair and body coverings. At various times in my life, I too have found it convenient, or respectful, to cover the hair and hide my body under full clothing. What is their reason for wanting to hide their eyes? Many of our men would support the idea that the most sexually attractive feature of a woman is the expression in her eyes!—it is where one sees an invitation that says, "I want to know you better." Yet, in the traditional burqa, the eyes are all anyone can barely still see through that grill. To our way of thinking, the free eyes with that total covering of the rest of the "package" just makes the woman even more sexually enticing.

But having given this some thought, I have come to the conclusion that we Canadians, men and women alike, are ourselves still hiding behind what I call our "invisible burqas." We seem to think so highly of the rules and mores, which our society has instilled that we may as well have the face covering ourselves. Perhaps we might even feel freer! How many times have you heard the admonition, "Don't do that! What will the neighbours say?" I grew up with it, and I am sure I am not alone. It could be about anything from picking your nose in public to making out with your boyfriend in the driveway after dark. Especially effective were the rules of the church. Most of us used to attend church regularly, and we feared the horrible consequences of going astray. We knew such sinners went to hell!

Many people today do not attend church regularly, or even belong to a religion. Many have come to the understanding that God is about LOVE, not revenge. He does not expect us to follow unquestioningly those manmade rules. He gave us the ability to reason, the freedom to make our own decisions, and to live our lives according to what we decide is right for us as individuals. Granted this freedom can lead to some awesome and awful messes, but then there is no god to blame for those results, only ourselves.

In my lifetime, I have made good friends with a lot of people who have met the challenges of living their lives the way they determined was right for them. In doing so, they also have made significant contributions to our world. They have realized that life is about loving God, and loving themselves, and loving the people one knows, and meets. Hence, this "new" thinking has led to empty churches, and conferences about that problem. Maybe the following pages will help these discussions.

The following sections tell the stories of my friends and family, and of how they have coped with life's trials. I hope as you read, you will think of other similarly successful lives you have known. The world and its population are really getting better. I have faith that these challenges and triumphs are what God wants for us! He loves us in spite of ourselves. Can you love this caring God, and decide for yourself which of the old scary rules are right for you to follow?

You Must Always Be as Physically Attractive as Possible

W hy? This was an important rule if you expected to attract a desirable mate, and don't you ever forget that the main purpose of your existence is to reproduce. How else could you get "good looking" and 'smart" genes for your children if you weren't attractive enough to "catch" the perfect partner?

I remember a guidance counsellor who joked to me that the successful men in business would choose the wives who really were physically attractive. They had forgotten to check out the women's brainpower! They then wondered why the child looked great, but failed in school. Perhaps the people who have arranged marriages, and who force the bride to wear burqas, may have a point. At least someone else has probably checked out the prospective partner! They must trust, however, the other person's judgement and wonder if that person had their best interest at heart. I wanted to practice my God given free will to make my own choice of a mate.

The desire to slavishly follow the idea that you should look only at a prospective partner's physical qualities has led to some pretty ridiculous pairings and situations. Little girls have been led to believe that, if they are beautiful they will all be married to prince charming, and live happily ever after. "Thank you, Walt Disney!" The saddest outcome of this idea are the adult wives who still believe that if they look good, and produce good looking offspring, their husbands will remain faithful. The worst result of this stress on appearance is the recent development of beauty contests for little girls. I saw an interview with a five-year-old who said that she had to lose weight and thought she would need to have a surgery on her face when she was older. What a false sense of values! What a miserable life she'll have if someone doesn't set her straight as to what is really important in life.

"Have you got time for a visit, or a coffee, or a time for a talk?" More than once, I've listened to the heartbreak of these wives who were slaves to their appearance, and other wifely duties. Many a man does not want to leave such service, but he can't leave his lustful mistress. She is one whom he says he "respects a lot." I n these cases of wifely distress, I could do nothing but listen. Inevitably he leaves, lives with the mistress, leaves the mistress, and before you know it, he wants the wife and all her free "services" back again. A mistress can be very expensive! Should the wronged wife agree to his return, she'll still need to be constantly reassured that she still looks attractive to this wanderer. The older we get, the harder that is! Will this couple be happy? What a challenge such a relationship can be, especially when there is no trust and no other bond of background, life goals, or beliefs.

Any person of either sex, who decides to get married because he/she has found an available gorgeous creature, really is a dunce! He/she is certainly not ready for any kind of a permanent relationship. As I used to advise any young people, who asked me, "Go out with the popular ones a few times. It's great fun to have the experience of "arm candy." I know whereof I speak. At college, I dated a handsome hockey player. It was good for my self-confidence.

People will say, "What a handsome couple you are." Don't fall for their admiration. Check out the brains, the character, and most importantly, the moral values. Does he/she respect, and really love the family who nurtured him/her? Now, we're into a lot of questions. Does he/she have a family worthy of all that love and respect? Is the person looking for a mother or a father? Is the fact that he/she are so good-looking scaring you away? Do you tend to think the "package" is too good to be true? I remember one boy telling me that he'd dated the girl who was the "best of the lot" and everyone else wanted her for a girlfriend. He dumped her the night after he went to her home to pick her up for a date, when he saw her being abusive to her mother. I really respected him for his decision. Maybe, you are wondering if the gorgeous person is too good to be true, but what if he/she is that perfect? If so, and there is that certain sexual tension, then go for it! Just be really sure you both feel that same desire to be together, and neither one is "using" the other.

I can't leave this topic of how you look without saying what the reality is. In our present society, looks do matter. There is no shame in doing what you choose to do to improve your appearance. People of both sexes are wrong if they figure that there is no need to look after themselves, and not to be as physically healthy as possible. Anyone who is neat, clean, and tidy is attractive, especially if there is a smiling face, and a happy attitude. One man told me he married his rather large wife because she was a lot of fun to be with. They'll soon celebrate their 20th anniversary, and they have a solid and healthy marriage and family.

My husband will often comment on a woman, call her pretty, even if he sees her as too heavy. He says it is her smile, or her actions, or maybe the proportions of her figure, which he found attractive. Men, more than women, tend to look at the whole "package." When some women see themselves in the mirror, they see only the fault they think they have, but not their assets. How many people love Oprah and think that she is beautiful, yet she is still fussing about that extra weight! My father had a little ditty that went: "My face I don't mind it as I am behind it; it is the people in front that I jar." If you think this way, love yourself, and have a great self -image, then others will see you through your eyes. It is true! You set the attitude for other peoples' opinion of you.

If you are in the dating scene, enjoy your time. Ignore the negative opinions of others. They may just be jealous of those great assets you have. Remember these years are the time when you have two jobs. You are to judge prospective partners, and to sort out the "losers" from the "winners." You are also supposed to be maturing into a person "worthy" of the type of person you want to be with! Begin this process by learning to love yourself.

Rule 2

You Must Have Socially Acceptable Behaviour

Being on one's best behaviour was always stressed when we were growing up. We were admonished to be sure to act like ladies and gentlemen, whether we were at home, or in public. "What will the neighbours say?" was said frequently. I think my mother felt that her reputation in the community depended on having her children socially well trained and under control. Also, she was conscious of the fact that my father was the school principal, and that his reputation might suffer should one of us do or say something which was not "acceptable."

There certainly were rules of behaviour, which were not to be questioned. Why? Well, if you learned and practiced them at home when it mattered less, you would do and say these things automatically when it "mattered" a lot. Then, you would not be embarrassed, and you would be accepted by the "right people." I can already hear many people of the present generation, laughing their heads off. "Who cares what others think?" is the present attitude. Such a rule as this came from our Anglo-Saxon background, and if you lived in present day England, you would care. Quite a few of the English, even now are very aware of the class system and its requirements. There are jobs you just would never get because of your lack of social training, and your background, or maybe your accent. Your education, and how gifted you were might be overlooked. There was a recent article about the fashions this year at the Ascot Races. It declared that one could tell the "ladies" from the "tarts" just by their choice of a proper hat. I'm afraid this is sad, but true.

Do proper behaviour and manners still matter in Canada? Some people from the area where I was raised might laugh and say, "Oh, 'social graces" only matter in Upper Canada!" In the Maritimes, we're not snobs, of course! I believe you could find humans beings you might personally consider to be 'snobs" if you looked under "any leaf." There will always be those who have been taught to think of themselves as superior.

I recently read an article saying that we are now raising children who falsely believe they are superior. We are letting our students never face the fact that failure is possible if they don't really try their best—it is too much praise in school for too little effort. Are 'manners" even stressed? That'll depend on the teachers and the thinking parents. We are hearing a lot now about bullying. Don't students who feel they are too superior, and who lack manners and compassion do that? Manners, if taught, might develop consideration at least. I heard "please" and "thank you" far more often when I was teaching in jail, than I did from students in regular schools.

It is a common misconception that good social skills are associated with being a snob. I have certainly been ridiculed for an action, or a way of talking that would have been expected behaviour in my home. I've learned to suit my manners to my audience, as most of us do adjust to the listeners nowadays. We have completely dropped a lot of usages. But I still expect the appropriate "please" and "thank you."

Before I discuss how social rules have changed with the passing of time, why do we even need any of them? How can you show compassion and concern to people if you obviously do not understand the other person's reactions and feelings? For some it is innate; for others, as I just said, it's a learned "gift."

Previously, gentlemen were to follow certain very strict rules. I was reminded of this when a young boy had his picture in a recent newspaper because he had received an award for bravery. He had seen a house on fire, and he had managed to save the lives of two younger children by pulling them out of the flames. When the interviewer commented on his actions, he just said, "It was what any gentleman would have done." I'm afraid I know a lot of adult males who would have had second thoughts about being that brave. This falls under the rule that gentlemen are expected to help the weak and the needy, because men are stronger, and because it is just the "right thing" to do. Saving a life would probably be an idea that most people still would accept as logical and acceptable social behavior. Most men really are physically stronger, but how about the rule that you never let a girl carry a heavy parcel if you are with her? Yeah! Just walk down any street and you'll see that idea does not apply.

My mother-in-law used to comment on what a fine gentleman my father was. He used to always: open doors for ladies, pull out chairs for ladies at the table, stand when a lady entered a room, tip his hat to a lady if he met her on the street, introduce a lady first, never speak ill of a lady, and on, and on. How much of this do you see today? He would never interrupt a person who was speaking. If he disagreed with the person, he would only be muttering a demur comment. These are the things that my grandsons are being taught in England. Women like all these. Most men in our present day don't even think of making these gestures. As a man, try some. You'll be surprised by the reactions. Maybe you'll get scolded by the feminists among us. Maybe, you'll gain a friend for life, or at least a wonderful smile.

What was a "lady" supposed to do "to pass muster" socially? We have just finished watching a TV programme called *Redemption*. Kevin O'Leary is a well-known Toronto financier. He had the idea of a show each week, in which he would finance and would help inmates turn their lives around once their sentences were served. Having worked in a jail and realized how many times we saw inmates return on new charges, I believe Mr. O'Leary is a saint. He gave them business challenges. The one who failed was dropped from the show. Each person who left would receive a financial package and lessons, which were designed to suit his interests and abilities. Those packages alone were expensive!

The final recipient got that package as well as the one hundred thousand dollars to assure her she could realize her dream. Yes, the winner was the only woman in the group. I tell you this story because she was so lacking in social graces. She was, however, so genuine that everybody loved her, even when she shocked them. You could see her weekly efforts to improve, and to do and say what she realized was expected. Each week she came closer to that goal, and she only swore once in the final episode!

Therefore, you know that a lady is expected never to swear in public. This is just the start of the list. My husband had a more liberal view of cleavage exposure than I ever did. I was taught ladies don't show skin except on a beach, and even then, very modestly. Fashions today and my daughter's generation have shown me that I was missing the boat. It appears that a lady should display her assets! In addition, ladies used to be seated properly with the legs crossed at the ankles and nothing above the knees showing. That was not hard for me, but if one had good legs, it wasn't fair! Ladies, of course never said anything nasty to, or about another person. Boy, that rule is gone. Did you hear the very public criticisms of the stars" dresses on the Academy Awards red carpet?

I've commented on a lot of the social rules and ideas which we have thrown out, but some very solid ones do remain. Never hurt another person intentionally. I find I can usually cause enough damage without trying. I talk too much! It is a social vice, or a nervous reaction, many of us have. It is hard to remember that although you may feel you really have much to contribute to a discussion, other people do too. Perhaps, we might even learn something . . . if we listened!

I also try not to swear, yet sometimes what I say can sometimes be thoughtless. Apologies are always in order. We are Canadians, eh? Once while skiing in Vermont, I was in a ladies washroom and bumped someone. I said, "Sorry," and the fellow skier said, "Oh, you are Canadian. You are all so polite." It's a good reputation, but hard to live up to. Importantly today, most of us are very socially aware of problems in society, and are quick to see what we can do to help. Any change for the better that one can affect, is most certainly following the "new rule": to have a kind and socially aware behavior. Both men and women have to be conscious that if, by using these old socially acceptable "rules", one is making another person feel uncomfortable; then that is wrong. Now, we should think of "good manners" as being anything said or done which makes the scene more comfortable for those in it. Remember if you don't love or aren't accepting yourself, then the result could be that you are not feeling like being loving and thoughtful to others.

Acts of caring and compassion are the best behaviour you can exhibit.

Rule 3

You Must Never Lose Emotional Control

When I was young, any display of emotion was regarded as lack of self-control. As my father said to me, "If you expect to control other people, to have them do what you wish, then you must first be in control of yourself." (Was that the philosophy that led to the British control of all the pink countries on our school maps?) I know it proved useful in teaching, but it was not great for personal development or relationships. Also, it can wreck havoc with your health. Emotions withheld have now become one of the factors suspected as causes of cancer, and certainly of mental health problems as well.

Although I learned not to vocalize my feelings, my mother had to frequently remind me that my face was too easily read. I could upset her just by looking at her. As I grew, I learned to keep as blank a face as possible. Now, I try to reflect in my face the emotions, which were being presented to me by the person to whom I am talking. That control has made me a person of whom others speak freely. I guess that was why I was reasonably successful when anyone came to me with a problem. I enjoyed the job of student counselling.

I did learn that in a classroom situation one must express displeasure at unacceptable behaviour. I soon learned which student reacted to a cross look, and which one needed sterner measures. I very seldom raised my voice, but when I used what I call the "teacher" voice, it was most effective. To be effective, it is important to make the sound short, loud, and deep, and never to screech. I'd be so in control that I could do that, and then turn to smile at the student who might have been upset by the outburst. That was obviously what my father had had in mind.

Yes, there are situations in which such emotional control is a useful skill. Just be sure that you are not feeling any upset in your own "gut." If so, then you are making yourself ill. It is hardest when you are dealing with your own child because you want so much to have him/her to become a perfect person. It becomes frustrating, especially if you have not yet realized that the aim of having a perfect child is hopeless. I found out that I had to wait to administer admonishment to my little girl. She caught on fast and knew the discussion of her behavior had to be delayed.

The result of this control is, of course, people I meet, and even some I know very well see me as a very calm individual. In a discourse, I give some input, but I mainly ask questions and listen to the answers. I know I've learned a lot that way. Yet, my really close friends, with whom I feel I am on the same wave length, will tell me that I never shut up. After an hour or two with such a friend, my throat will be sore. I am very fortunate to have many of these people around me, and within reach by phone. No, I don't rely on the internet as I need to hear the tone of voice. I have used Skype with various degrees of success.

Now, that is all the positives of self-control in regards to feelings. What about the negatives?

When two people I know are shouting and fighting with each other, I leave the space, the room, the area, or whatever. I just try to get as far away as possible. If I can't leave, then my stomach begins to pain, and then I make every effort to play the moderator. This is, of course, not what they want. They wish only to make sure that the other person(s) know(s) exactly how they personally think and feel. I often wonder if they really do feel better after having done that. Does it really feel good to express your anger?

Whenever I tried this as a child, I was sent to my room and told not to reappear until I had a happy face. I could stay a long time. If I had felt justified anger, and if when I returned, I tried to explain that I was the wronged party, I was not listened to. My face might have looked "happy", but my head was not! It did not make for my good feelings toward the sibling who had hit me, or had taken my toy. My mother had peace. Yet these feelings do build up over time. I was fed up with the excuse, "You are the oldest, and you must set the example."

These personality "difficulties" really come to the fore when you mate with a person whom you expected was "raised the same", and who you thought would have the same ideas about self-control. I did not. Divorce was never an option, the plan was to stay married "until death do us part." That was how it was in the fifties. The result was our long pairing and a lot of adjusting for both. It was a good thing we were in love and a long way away from family influences. We had to work out the differences by ourselves. I was often uptight, and I felt that pain in the stomach more than once. Keeping my mouth closed saved a lot of fights. I learned to accept many things. My husband would probably say, "me too!"

We had eight years to adjust to each other before we had a child. We were in love. We had a lot of trips and fun times playing at being adults, having parties and going out with friends. My father had told me that I was so lucky to have such a good man, and I was never to try to change him. My mother had agreed that he was wonderful, so I believed the problems were mine. I looked around at other couples with whom we were friends, and the situation was identical. As one of the female friends said to her husband, "You decide, and I abide." So, I thought that was life.

Things changed when there was a child. We had very different ideas about how to handle discipline. I guess we had both mellowed, and my husband was away a lot so I had the chief parenting role in the home. She is now an independent, successful lady. I'm glad that I tried not to stifle her, as I had been.

Yes, emotional control has a place in everyone's life. It does make relationships smoother. I like the motto from the AA groups. Change what you can, accept what you can't, know the difference! Try to calm down and express displeasure positively, lovingly, and quietly! In other words, if the relationship can't be altered, leave. Don't stay around complaining and making yourself emotionally ill.

Rule 4

You Must Watch Your Language

This rule started early with . . . all children should be seen, not heard. Always listen respectfully when the adults are speaking, especially if you are getting a lecture! Never say anything to criticize, or hurt anyone. Keep your voice down in any public place. Ladies, particularly, never speak loudly. Always use the best grammar you've been taught . . . And never, never, never ever use bad words, or use God's name in a disrespectful manner. In retrospect, it is a wonder that we ever learned to talk!

Most of us who were raised this way have noticed that more and more modern parents have realized that children do have talking rights, and will learn to use the language better if they are allowed to actually speak. It leads to some interesting situations and noise that, we as adults, would rather not hear. Most of us who have had children understand that their talking is an important part of the learning process. Parents can, however, get some pretty dirty looks when in public. "Dad, isn't that a crazy idea that mom was telling me? She said she had a baby in her tummy!" If you take that child to church for a long and boring service be prepared for outbursts of honesty. At the end of a long family service, the youngest niece said very loudly and clearly what we were all thinking, "Well, finally!"

Once, when we were attending a new church, the minister's wife told me she would miss the service next week and look after our child if we wanted to attend. Disapproval of children's talking is particularly true now in many denominations where people are just about all grey and bald. Then we wonder why the "freer" churches have more people attending, especially younger families. The popular churches have learned to have children's services with "entertainment." My nephew, who attends one, has recently been volunteered to make an ark so that the story of Noah could be dramatized. It all harkens back to the days of the old cathedrals, when no one could read, and the dramatizations were common. Apparently, they even used to flood some of those old buildings for that story! I was told that by the guide when I visited Notre Dame in Paris.

The grammar lessons in the home have really fallen by the wayside. "We do not use that language in this house. The word "these" is plural if followed by a plural verb. We say "these" houses, not "them" houses." My mother had been a teacher. Not even an English teacher in a school today would correct a student in that fashion, especially not for that particular rule. I must say, however, I still find it grates when I hear a misuse. The words "fewer" and "less" are frequently confused. I have even seen that mistake in the Globe and Mail. ("Fewer is for items that can be counted, "less" is for those that can't.) How's that for being archaic? English is a growing language and we must adapt, but I would still like complete sentences and subjects that agree with their predicates.

I dread to think what the results of texting must be doing to the essay writing. One can only expect the poor computer to do so much correcting.

If a person, as a child, has never been allowed to argue, then as an adult, he/she will find it difficult to defend his/her actions or opinions. We were told to go to our rooms until we had a happy face. I realize it made our parents' lives pleasanter, but we learned that our opinions were not valuable. The usual line was that, "I have lived longer and have had more experience and you must trust me." How many parents use this line when they themselves are uncertain, or out of control? Isn't that the philosophy by which the German nation got into so much trouble? I have a friend who grew up in that horrid situation. It was not until 1947 that he understood its real horror. Since it was recognized that he was a bright boy, he was selected after the Second World War, to go to a special school on one of the islands in the German Baltic. There the students were to be educated for leadership positions in the new German Republic. He says that the majority of the teachers were of the old school, and preached the doctrine of the superiority of the Arian race. Their students were to accept what they were told.

One history teacher saved this child's life. By the time the boy was fourteen, this teacher could see that my friend was a reflective person. He showed this student an old New York Times newspaper he had saved. The paper, of course, had a different point of view! Obviously, an intense discussion was involved. The young boy then resolved to get as far away from Germany as he could. He stowed away on a ship and got to England, and thence to Canada. Then, he felt Halifax was not far enough from Germany, so he rode the rails to Vancouver. There he worked on a farm. He was gradually able to educate himself to the level of a master's degree. When he was earning a living, he married and raised a family. The children were encouraged to form opinions, and discuss ideas with their parents.

I know children should be encouraged to think and express their ideas. How else are they going to develop their own sense of values? For example, when you discuss your ideas with the youngest ones, they learn why following blindly is wrong. They learn why being selfish, stealing, and other wrongs against their friends are wrong. They can thus hope to grasp the concept of compassion. Teens also really need to talk with older people to test the new values they are considering, values encouraged by their peers. These ideas are not necessarily all wrong. This is how the world progresses. We old fogies might thus learn something. I was told many times that marijuana should be legalized; now it is in a couple of American states.

Another idea regarding language is the "no dirty" words rule. "What is a 'dirty' word?" My mother's favourite word was *sxxt*. It was only used in "emergencies." Hence, it has become mine. I guess it was perhaps our grandmother's, as I have discovered that it is what my cousin says as well. Once in front of a Grade 9 class (a good and "tame" class) I used it! I was wearing a new light summer suit and, as usual, waving a red pen around as I gesticulated. The open pen hit the front of the skirt and the inevitable happened! Even at the end of the year, one little girl said to me, "miss, do you remember that day you said *sxxt*?"

Obviously the definition of "dirty word" depends on one's culture and upbringing. It seems many of us believe that, in usage, modern language has no boundaries, and the most common word is the four-letter one, which is used as any part of speech one needs. Consequently, it can appear several times in one sentence! When I taught and later volunteered in jail, I became immune to it; it was just floating around in the air. If I were talking to an inmate through the bars, and he heard it, the inmate would often apologize to me, saying, "Miss, I'm sorry you have to hear that."

That word, which I can't use here for obvious reasons, is really fairly innocent. Most people don't even know it is just the initials for on old criminal charge that applied to sailors in the British Navy years ago. It used to be illegal for the sailors to engage in homosexual activity. (*For Uncommon Carnal Knowledge*)

The swearing that really upsets me is the usage of God's name. Whatever your religion, or your religious words, there is no excuse for that. God does not deserve such dishonour when he is the one who gives you unconditional LOVE. He does not make the world's misery. Misguided humans and natural forces cause the suffering we endure. No religion can believe that the horror we are now seeing in Syria was caused by their idea of God.

The worst language of all is the use of words, which are designed to criticize and to make the other person feel inadequate, and consequently feel pain. There is nothing harder for a child to hear than the words, which tell him/her that he/she is unloved and unwanted. How many adults do this without a thought? Sarcasm is often used by teachers as their specialty to control their class. Parents can also do this, thoughtlessly, especially if they are tired or drunk. Such nasty comments can also be the result of the person's past, and can be the effort to make the speaker feel superior. How insecure are you when you have to make yourself feel superior by putting a child down?

My mother's old admonition does apply "Put your brain in gear before using your mouth!" Show compassion and love instead—especially to yourself. Take a break when you reach that stage of frustration. Been there. It is easier said than done.

Rule 5

You Must Have a University Education

I have two degrees from the University of New Brunswick. All my siblings have degrees, so does my husband and so did all his siblings, and so does my daughter. It was just a given. My mother-in-law's greatest possession was the framed photo of all her children in their caps and gowns. Did we all have happy and productive lives because of our degrees? Well, not exactly. The question really is "Did formal education lead to our having more self-fulfilling and happier lives?" That is not for me to say!

My own maternal grandmother had some education. She was qualified, probably she had Grade 10. She worked as a teacher for many years before her marriage. Once she married, she was forbidden to do so because in those times it was felt that she'd be taking a job from a man. I'm not sure if that was perhaps even a law. Her society believed that a married woman should be supported by her husband, and that working for money would hurt her husband's ego. That was my own mother's philosophy. In later life, she agreed to teach only after my father retired. They had been teachers with one year's normal school training. Later my father earned a couple of university degrees, on his veteran's loan, in summer school and by studying at night. They'd met when she moved to a school where he was the principal. It was a big 'secret" that they liked each other . . . until they came back from the Christmas holiday as a married couple. She taught only to the end of June that school year.

My maternal grandfather had carpenter's training and a business certificate. He had a successful business and a productive life, and was well respected in his town. Yet, there is a situation, which I heard of where a young man is being discouraged for taking up carpentry as a career choice.

My other grandparents finished high school. My grandmother was training to be a nurse, but was sent home when it was discovered that she'd been nursing a couple of sailors who had died of small pox. That was in the early twentieth century. She then went to work in her future husband's store. He was successful there and he had success in running a number of lumber mills.

My husband's parents had formal education to the end of Grade 10, which was all that was offered in rural Nova Scotia when they were young. My mother-in-law was terribly embarrassed if anyone found out that she had done housework before marriage. All her life she wrongly envied those whom she felt knew more than she did, just because they'd been in school longer. She had a most acquisitive brain and knew far more than I did about all household matters. Thank God, that in Canada we now have universal high school education. People no longer must live with this embarrassment.

My father-in-law was a wonderful man. His life was challenging and interesting. He and his brother operated a lumber business. They could provide well for their families. When my father-in-law died, many, many people came to pay their respects. He was so loved and valued in his community that the comments still bring tears to my eyes. Men, who felt that they did not have proper clothes for the funeral, came in their lumbermen's attire to shake my husband's hand at 'the wake." They said things such as "You never knew, but my family would have starved one winter if it hadn't been for your father's kindness. Did you know that your father could lift over his head a barrel which weighed more than he did?" What a wonderful and productive life he had! He was respected and loved by all who knew and worked with him.

I guess you can see where I'm going with this 'must have a degree rule." Yes. I am very glad I went to university. Originally, I planned to use my education to become a social worker. I was discouraged in that by my parents. I persisted and took a lot of psychology courses. I loved those classes. I even went so far as to apply for government assistance to go to McGill for postgraduate training. The man in charge of "the deciding" refused me. My marks were good enough. The problem was, and he told me: "You would probably get married and not use the government sponsored training!" I then took university courses at my home university to become a teacher. Probably I was more successful than I would have been as a social worker. I'll never know. I do know I loved my students, and found the profession challenging, and fulfilling, especially with pupils who appreciated my love and attention.

I was recently reminded of this idea of the necessity of a degree by an article in the National Post. The writer, William Watson, was commenting on the fact that students in Quebec had planned to strike because their government was thinking of raising tuition fees. Their tuition rates for college and university courses are now the lowest in Canada. Their government changed and their tuition stayed the same. Were they right? In Germany, there is no tuition for the students who qualify and maintain their grades. Their economy appears to have benefitted. Is that a better idea? Watson agreed that some of the students did have huge debts when they finished their degrees. Yet, statistically considered, he said the degree does mean more money over a person's lifetime. It is not, however, true for all professions. I was fortunate to be a teacher in my epoch, and not in my father's. In the "old days" there were no unions or federations. I now have a comfortable pension and a worry free retirement. He did not. He had to take another job when he retired, and he worked at that until he was much older. Fortunately, the choices which he made did lead to his very productive and happy life. The existence and power of many unions is now under threat as they have outreached their grasp, financially. Again, I was blessed.

The point is, that university is not right for everyone. Would it have improved my father-in-law's life? I do not believe it would have. He seemed happy when he was at his business, and so were the many grateful men and women whom he hired. Can one really ask for more of life? I know of many young people today who wish for only that satisfaction. But there are so many graduates today who can't even find employment with their "mortgaged" degrees. They would gladly settle for such a productive life. We have not done them any favours by stressing university attendance. I know young successful men and women in the trades. They are carpenters, plumbers, operators of businesses, such as those in construction. They have much more interesting lives, and more respect than those unhappy degree people in jobs, which are not challenging. No one is sadder than a young girl I know who believed she had to live up to her father's expectations, and finish a degree. The pressure was usually greater when the parent did not himself/herself go to university. If you recognize yourself in this situation, get off the bandwagon. Take charge of your life. Ask yourself what it is that you really want to do. What gives you a feeling of joy, what do you find rewarding? Do that! You only have one life, right?

I am so proud of two of my close male relatives. Their older siblings both have degrees and they started to follow the brothers' paths at university. They had even completed a lot of university courses. Then the first boy stopped and just told himself that it was not "his way." He realized that he had been in love with airplanes since his stint in Air Cadets. Thus, he became an air traffic controller. The other one realized that the outdoors was his milieu and he became a farmer. Are they leading lives, which they consider more satisfactory? Yes. Both now have time for chosen recreations: motorcycle adventures and curling, as well as more time than they might have had for their families.

In view of the philosophy I've been advocating, this falls under the category of "love yourself." Let yourself be happy with your life choices. Then, you will be prepared to love and care for yourself and for your fellow human beings.

You Must Have Money for Security

I t was an understood idea that you had your education so you could earn as much money as possible, and then you and your family would have a pleasant life as well as a secure old age. The people in my generation had grandparents who lived through the depression in Canada. My mother remembered it well. When I visited my parents, and they were older, one job I did was to empty the dishes in the refrigerator. Often the food was all the little bits of leftovers. Some of them would be mouldy! My father-in-law had been really ill once from eating the fish which he had left in a tin can. It was, to that generation, a sin to waste any food. He and my grandfather knew what it was to walk miles to work in the thirties. They both said they felt lucky to have those jobs at a dollar or two a day. Hence, I learned that being thrifty was a virtue. I remember my mother's Aunt Lou, telling me that the men used to choose wives for their ability to peel a potato so that the least skin was removed. That proved she'd be thrifty.

This problem of worrying about living to an old age without money is again causing some concern. People my age group have been living in a paradise we didn't even appreciate. During our working lives there was no depression, no war, and we had a good opportunity for a relatively cheap education. We now have good pensions, and the present governments have provided abundantly for our financial assistance. It looked so good that the generation behind us thought that they could depend on the government aid. Many did not save; they just enjoyed their money. Now, as the federal parliament realizes its folly and discusses cuts to these support programmes, the present generation is panicking.

When one realizes that at present there are more people living to older ages, and that more people are living in our country, the problem should have been obvious. Those who used their heads thought about this. For the people who have never saved, this old rule about saving is relevant. They had better start now. They shouldn't hope that their parents, who are in my age bracket, will leave their savings to them just because they are their offspring. There is a humorous ad on TV, which shows the younger adults becoming upset because the older people are spending money as if the source of that river would never run dry. Don't they have the right to do as they chose with their own savings? We are! Our daughter knew that we had the responsibility to make sure that she was equipped to earn a good living. It was, as my mother had emphasized to me; she told me not to expect to have a husband for financial support. Life is too uncertain.

In Canada, we have done a great disservice to some of our girls to lead them to believe that they will have a life of leisure once they "catch a husband." Some expect that as long as the children are small the husband will always work and bring home the only pay cheque. Many women have experienced that unpleasant surprise as he walked out the door. It also bothers me a lot to hear of the single mothers who expect the government to supply the welfare on which they will raise children. I recall the comment I heard "I'm having another baby so welfare will give me a new apartment with another bedroom." What kind of a life will those children have?

Once one's family has basic security, there is another side to this problem. Just how much money is needed so one can believe that the family will be well looked after, and will feel secure?

One of the saddest things I see now is the older couples who have the money, and who won't enjoy it once they have enough to live comfortably. Does it just sit in the bank at low interest? There is no fun, no travel, and no satisfaction of helping others. They lived in the era before public health care, and still have that spectre hanging over their heads. How many people spend their old ages this way? "What we will be doing in ten years' time?" is a favourite topic when we get together with friends. It is almost as popular a topic as our health problems!

One hears comments such as "Oh, I'm saving all my money for the children and the grandchildren." Why would you be doing that? Are those younger people disabled? If so, it's a good reason. What about the following excuse: "Oh, but my son is afraid that I might have an accident if I went away." Is he really worried about you, or that you'll not leave the money you might spend for him? Another common thought is "my money is tied up in my house and I want to leave that to the children. I know it's hard to keep up, and a lot of work for me." Are you sure they even want the old place? Is that really stopping you from moving to a place where you'd be safer, and have more comforts?

The children should usually understand that the money which is left when you go may be their inheritance. That includes the price of the house you sold! It is, however, the property of the partner who is left at the other's death. That one, usually the wife, has the charge of the money and, if she is mentally alert, should do her own thinking and deciding, and not be talked into doing only what the "kind" advisors tell her. Yes, I am sarcastic. She may have her own favourite charities, and her charities may not be her children who have abused her! The real "horror" for the children comes when the person left behind happens to form a new relationship. You wouldn't get married again . . . would you? That is the parent's decision, and a loving child would want him/her to be happy. The money does not have to go to his/her offspring!

Should we save any money beyond what is required immediately and for the foreseeable future? Yes, as I said earlier, life is uncertain. Things happen. We have just seen the devastation of the tornadoes in the USA. If such natural disasters should happen here, ready cash would be a Godsend. However, would you honestly need to keep holding a million just in case of a crisis? You might need some extra if you lived in many other countries, how about in United States right now? Is not this the extra money that the one percent protesters were bothered about? Didn't they realize that such money is usually invested in businesses, which provide the engines of our economies, and hence jobs?

The extra money can be justified if one is running a business and the finances are required for that. It is especially true if you have many employees, and you are constantly meeting the payroll. You must make sure that any money you decide to keep extra is productive money, and to do that is work. If it is not your own business, and you are retired, then it must be invested properly so those companies and utilities whose shares you have are productive. I am retired. My husband continues to do this work.

Maybe you prefer to invest any extra money in a charity, which is really investing in the lives of people who are struggling. In this case, it is a lot harder to determine the effectiveness of the use or your money. Maybe, you'll get a picture of the child you have sponsored. Maybe, you'll see on TV the work of the

"*Doctors without Borders*" in a disaster zone. Maybe, you will have a personal connection to a charity in Africa. We did. There was a nursing programme in Mozambique that our church heard wherein they needed a truck to take nurses to pregnant mothers. Our church raised the cash, and we could send it directly to the mission station. There was no middleman. There is a white truck in Africa with our church's name on it.

Unfortunately, it has become obvious lately that some organizations, which ask for money, benefit the organizer more than the people they claim to help! Be sure to check thoroughly, and note the percentage of received money that goes to the office overhead.

In conclusion, once you are financially secure, extra money is a responsibility. Be as wise as you can. Everybody has to decide for him/herself. It is not easy to know what is right. My Dad thought we could all support ourselves so he got rid of as much extra cash as he could, and had his own ideas about where it should go! He left only the tax receipts. Was he right? Among other projects, he sponsored many, which were related to promoting a sustainable environment for his descendants. His money did a lot of good.

God gave us the right and the ability to make decisions— use this great gift wisely. In most countries in the world, you'd be lucky to just have enough money for food, let alone for health concerns. You are indeed blessed to live in this country. I'm typing this on Canada Day!

Rule 7

You Must Remember Lust Is Bad

Recently the Pope of the Catholic Church read the Riot Act to his disobedient clergy. He made it very clear that they were in big trouble if they persisted in wanting to ordain women clergy. Imagine the poor fellow male priests, and the temptations they'd have to fight if they had to work alongside female priests! The real horror that the Pope stressed was that some of the clergy were suggesting that they should have a personal choice about celibacy. Imagine the problems of having a married priest. They might love their wives more than God and their congregation . . . Yet, why not have married clergy? Most other religions do think that women are acceptable to God as marital partners or even as clergy.

The church's fear of lust would appear to be the Pope' reasoning. A married priest might experience lust for his wife A woman among those unmarried priests might tempt them t

feel lust. The irony, of course, is that the lust of these currently frustrated priests is at present ruining the Catholic Church. The number of people, whom I've heard say that they used to be Catholics is very large. They don't even say why they left, just the facial expression says it all. Hypocrisy doesn't sell!

So what is this monster called 'lust' of which the church is so afraid? The Canadian Oxford has two definitions. The first definition is, "strong sexual desire." This is precisely what the Pope fears, and sexual lust is what all "good" members of the Catholic clergy hope to be able to suppress throughout their lives. If this is good, why did God tell Abraham to go forth and multiply? The joys of sex, and the resulting babies, are the greatest of God's blessings. The popes in former years had many mistresses and children. They were able to endow them with many privileges, such as asking a son, "Would you like to be the priest in this particularly rich area?" The idea of men priests is perhaps based on the fact that Jesus had only men as the twelve apostles. Is it the thought that Jesus didn't trust women? That is false. If He didn't have women as disciples, where did the gospel of Mary Magdalene come from? Why was it that only the women went to the tomb and saw Jesus first? Any prejudice against women priests presents many incongruities.

Can this lust for the joy of sex get out of control and cause problems? You bet! We are physically programmed to reproduce at a very early age. This was fine when we all were grandparents at age forty. Now, we hope to get enough education to support ourselves to at least the age of seventy. Thus those ambitions will be thwarted if one has three children by the time he/she is the age of twenty-one. I know that I, as a teen, was very aware of living with this sexual tension; I understand and I do feel a lot of sympathy for teenagers. It is now known that men at any age think of sex far more often than do females. I had one man, not too young, who told me that he could be in the most important

business meeting, and still there would be one part of his brain working on the possibilities of sex. I like the expression which I heard one father tell his son, "masturbate, don't impregnate."

If you were told that the chief function of existence was to go forth and multiply, then maybe you got the idea that any other form of release for sexual tension was evil. Again, remember the admonishment in the Old Testament was meant for the numerical increase of the tribe of Israel. I believe today that God would not think that any unwanted child, one who will not be loved, is a good idea.

The "pill" is a recent and most appreciated invention, but it did mean that all of a sudden one no longer had to be celibate for fear of an unwanted pregnancy. This fear is what kept my generation relatively "honest." We couldn't trust the available birth control methods. There was many a bride who wore the white dress down the aisle to the music of the whispers of the gossips. The girls who lived in the out ports in Newfoundland were luckier. It was well known that one could not be expected to wait for the minister who came only once a year when the ice was out of the harbor. When he arrived he was a busy boy. (Note: no women priests.) He then had all the funerals, christenings, and marriages to perform. It wasn't uncommon for the first child to be a flower girl or a ring bearer, and the mother to be in the final stages of the pregnancy for the next child. I know of a true case in which a minister did the service while the labor pains for the second baby were happening.

This total freedom from convention and religious belief has its drawbacks. (We must remember also that the third world has no such a "pill" privilege.) Are we using it wisely? Here are some things to consider. What about the man who never ever even plans to marry, but considers that his lot on life was to keep all the women he meets "happy"? What about the women we hear of now with the same philosophy The threat is that they will have a lonely old age—will they? It is not necessarily so. What if the woman planned on the traditional family life, had all the "blessings" of a "proper" marriage, and then had no children? In addition, men statistically die earlier. Often their widows chose to have long lonely years. In the old days, spinsters were pitied. Older single women are not.

I heard just yesterday of a teacher who took his pension just after a few years of work, and went off to the USA and made fortunes in real estate. He lived the high life and rubbed shoulders with the rich and famous. When that market went bust, he returned to Canada to teach again. When I asked what he thought he had contributed to the good of the world, the reply was that he was a great teacher. He did a lot to help his students gain self-confidence. He will never have the love of a child he raised himself. Will he miss that? One of God's great gifts is the freedom to choose our own path in life. Stop and consider. Are you happy with the path you've chosen, or did lust get you into trouble?

Being married does not guarantee a happy and secure old age. Many marriages end in divorce. I'm not against marriage. Just be sure you are mature and that you are "your own" person before you exercise your right to decide on a marriage you believe will be permanent.

There is, according to the Oxford Dictionary, a second definition. It is the lust, or coveting, for material possessions. As a child, you may have been wishing for the toys, which a sibling received for Christmas, which you didn't receive. If the parents are not quick to talk about this feeling, and instruct about the value of feeling happy for others, it can lead to all sorts of problems later in life. It is not uncommon to hear the expression, "mom loved you better!" Beware, it is almost impossible for a parent not to engender those jealous feelings sometimes, and they should be addressed when they surface.

Is this where the desire to acquire things comes from? Is it just a need to make one's self feel superior? Perhaps, it is almost as if pleasing the parent is secondary to some innate need for security. Insecurity can lead to the belief that enough is never enough. Concerning material goods, that fear can be real; this world is not a stable place.

I do not have an answer to these questions. I guess it would be a good field for psychological study. I just know that this form of lust has caused a lot of heartaches. It's the root of the many problems I saw with inmates in jail. Granted, that most of them did actions to gain something, actions that they thought they could get away with for one last time. Many also really had no other choice because of the drive to get funds for the drugs they wanted. Some, who were very dangerous, really had such severe psychological problems that they did not even know what they were doing. Yet, when I heard the word, "want", I realized that it was usually a case of covetousness, a lust for material things.

Once we had classroom help from a well-paid teacher who was charged with credit card fraud. She wanted to live better. It is interesting that the crimes of lust for material possessions often seem to be perpetrated by people who already have goods a bit beyond that which the rest of us possess. It seems they are ambitious to gain to keep up with someone else. Envy and its cousin, lust are indeed green-eyed monsters! You can really see this when you read the obituaries in the Report on Business. Yes, they were great financial successes. What good does that do them now? You see high school girls who live to be able to acquire more expensive brand name jeans. You see it when new parents buy the most expensive stroller for the new baby. Those people want the stroller, not the infant, but for the prestige that will impress their friends.

Where does this desire to impress people come from? Do you really need a much larger home, car, farm, or a sexier and younger wife? Are you so insecure that what other people think determines your own self-worth?

I said earlier that there is nothing wrong in our society with the idea that you wish to live comfortably. You should be able to do that in Canada if you have a job, and live within your means. Being good to yourself and to your community should gain you a place of security, a place where you have comfortable and friendly relations with others. If you live only for yourself, and are not helpful to others, then you will have a very lonely life.

I am reminded of a real story of an old man who was mean to the children in his small community. I would not want to have been in his shoes on Halloween night. The children in their disguises tormented him unmercifully. Was he mentally ill, or was it just that he couldn't share joy with other people; he couldn't even be kind to little ones.

Yes. Beware of lust, which causes you to be unkind to others. It does come back to "bite you." Life is so much pleasanter when you control your lust and are just loving and thoughtful toward others. This presupposes that you love yourself as Jesus directed us to do.

Do you sincerely want more friends, friends who want to hear your stories, and have fun with you? If so, the expression of jealousy and greed that is written in your eyes when you are near these people does drive them away, or at least make them very leery of being your confidant.

If you love yourself, it shines through, and makes others want to be with you, to be your friend. Be kind. Don't try to make others feel inferior. Beware of any expression of your hurtful lust.

Rule 8

You Must Get Legally Married

When I finally got married at the ripe old age of 23, my mother was very relieved, and she then turned her attention in doing the same for my two younger sisters. That was her job. Fortunately, life intervened. They were older, and later they were not living at home where she could "work on the problem." They did marry, but only in their late twenties, and each one totally made her own choice.

What a different scene it is today. The educated young girls, whether in college or working, do not feel the same pressure. Now, it seems even if you do not have the ability to support yourself and a child, it is not a problem should you chose to carry a pregnancy to full term. God bless the pill. If you did not live in our era, you have no idea what a great threat unwanted pregnancy was, and hence the pressure to be married. There were even girls naive enough to think that pregnancy was a way to "trap" a husband. It worked sometimes! There was always this threat . . . how can you even consider a child when you don't have a husband to financially support you? Abortions were only of the "back alley" type. I remember hearing of an older neighbor lady who almost bled to death because she decided she couldn't have the child. There were already more children than she could feed and house.

Today, one rarely hears of the other old concern: that a child deserves two parents! It used to be that you weren't supposed to work after marriage. Mothers stayed home. I had had a job for seven and a half years and I was accustomed to earning my own money. I had made the assumption that I always would work; my pregnancy was a happy surprise. As a young baby, our daughter was certainly not easy. I suspect that it was mostly my fault as I was sure I was doing everything wrong. Does that sound familiar to anyone? Neighbors were helpful, but strangers and my mother would just say, "She's yours. You'll do it by instinct. It's not my place to give advice." God bless Dr. Spock! My daughter was luckier when she was expecting because the new books were even more specific and useful.

One of my closest friends had a daughter and the father was not interested in being a parent, so he just gave her the money to have an abortion. That cash was placed in the educational fund. What a lot of joy that man missed! How deprived those grandparents were! The baby girl was and is very beautiful. When she was older, she even earned money by modelling. That helped with her university expenses. This girl's proud mother and stepfather attended her university graduations and walked her down the aisle at her wedding. She not only can earn a huge salary, but she, likewise, is also an excellent mother to her three gorgeous and bright children. Keeping that baby was the difficult, but the correct choice for my friend. She and her husband now have the gift of bright and loving grandchildren.

The Atlantic Monthly magazine of November 2011 carried an article on this topic. It was titled "All Single Ladies" and was written by Kate Bolick. The point was that not only do men have choices, but also the women have been "released" by "the pill." Girls are just as free as men to look around for the perfect mate and "try out a few" before settling down. It used to be that the woman might not even have a chance to decide, but be told by her parents that they felt this man was a good husband choice for her. It might be his money, or his social status that influenced the parental decision. The girl, in some cases, was lucky, and the prospective partner was a kind and good man. How often did that happen? I knew of one such case where the man was very lazy and not bright. The wife, who was my friend, had that "load" until her death. As one of my older widowed girlfriends says, "Why should I choose to look after another old man?" Yet, some older women are choosing to remarry. That must be what real love is!

It was understood in my time that one was to be married while it was still possible to have children. I remember a Grade 9 student from long ago. She was very innocent, pretty, and bright. In June, the other girls in the class told me how envious they were of her as she would be married next month. The man had built her a beautiful new house. They said they thought that it was a great thing. She'd be marrying an older man, and she would never have to go to school again. What happened? Was the man good to her? Did she have ten children? Was the house all that important? I changed schools and never found how it all turned out.

There are poor girls in India who must have arranged marriages; arranged even before they reach puberty, and often it is to older men. There are even girls who didn't see the man until the day of the wedding. Was he ugly as sin, and was he a nasty looking, mean person as well? Once on a plane I saw two girls from India. They were wearing their gorgeous saris and were heading for Toronto. They were very pretty teens and so excited.

Were they already married? Were they just going to meet their new husbands? I often wondered about their new lives in Canada. There are also girls who are in polygamous marriages and know nothing else. Now, in Canada (except in bountiful, B.C.), women have the right to choose their husbands. Do they always know that? Is that always true? Lately we heard of an older brother whose father convinced him that it was his duty to kill his sister because she had provocative pictures on the internet, and had a boyfriend. They lived within ten kilometres from my house. Thank goodness for Christie Blatchford, and the wonderful job of reporting these evils, which she has done.

The article by Ms. Bolick, said that because of our freedom of choice, the average age for females to marry has risen by six years to twenty-six. We girls realize that the more education we have, the better are our choices of a compatible mate. Suddenly, we realize that the trouble is the eligible men, the age of the educated women are very rare birds! Many younger men have heard the call of Mother Nature's sexual drive and wedded earlier.

The remaining men seem to go merrily on their ways like Johnny Appleseed and "spread the cheer around." They believe the old saying "If you can get the milk for free, don't buy the cow." The women now have a similar attitude. Here's a hint: it involves buying a pig. This was a phenomenon, which was first documented in other cultures, noticeably among the black males. I remember one of my students in jail telling me that he planned to have forty children. When I suggested that his wife would get very tired, the whole class broke into gales of laughter. "No, Miss, I mean *forty* baby mothers!" He was serious, since in his culture, that also was considered a test of his manhood.

I should mention also the fact that men who were never married, or never have formed a permanent relationship will statistically die long before the men with a caring partner. Maybe they will die happier. As when one looks at the older people, the men have the sad faces. There is no one to visit them. If you are a man who decided to remain single, get a dog. You will at least have a better chance to be healthier . . . maybe even happier than you would have been with some of the women to whom you took a fancy!

Research that was published recently showed that the children raised in lesbian homes (married or not) were the best adjusted. Now, before you get your "knickers in a knot," remember that a loving father and mother were next in line . . . a very close second. The article to which I referred, stressed the point that if a person decided to raise a family on his/her own, success depended on the constant support of an extended family. It was true even if that support was given by those who were not biologically related to the mother and child. What mattered was the love. My friend who kept her little girl had wonderful, loving family and friends', support. Hence we are back to God is LOVE, and that's what matters, as it makes all things possible.

Yes, get married, or not, as you both decide. It is your free will to do what you believe is right for you. Don't be influenced by those around you. Don't get married because everyone else is having a wedding. Don't get married if you thought it would never happen to you, and finally were asked! Don't get married because your unwanted baby needs a father. Worse things can happen! Most of the married people you talk to, will give you a lot of advice. The ideas will depend on their own experiences. You are not they! The "good" marriages last. Why? I think it is because both persons have verbally, or intrinsically, agreed to overlook each other's shortcomings, and have decided they can live with those faults. It is a big help if you can honestly say you love each other. I have been married for 52 years and I still love him a lot!

My hope for you is that, if you do decide to marry, and you really, really love each other, know each other very well before you decided to be together permanently. It will also help to have a shared set of values, similar backgrounds, and both feel a good dose of sexual desire such that you can't keep your hands off each other. Go for it! There will probably be no regrets.

Rule 9

Males Must Be the Head of the Family

I n my Anglo-Saxon culture, the father's total authority was an understood concept. Should he die before his time, it was the responsibility of the eldest son to both financially and emotionally support his mother and his younger siblings. Recently, I met a man who had had to do that. His father had died early and there were two younger sisters. He'd left school and gone to work. His sister, my friend, was celebrating her eightieth birthday. Her brother is now eighty-seven years old, and he had driven to her party. Thus, you know that times have changed for our culture within just the last seventy years. In some cultures, this idea of the eldest brother's responsibility is still the rule.

At the moment, this is particularly relevant as the trial and sentencing for a murder of family members by other family members is in the news. It is not the first time it has happened in Canada, but there were four persons killed this time, not just the one delinquent daughter. The reason given was that it was an "honor" killing. The father believed that he had to do it as his three girls were not "proper" young ladies, and one of his two wives had aided and abetted their behavior. In his culture, not in his religion, girls had to be kept under wraps until the suitable husband was found, by their father. They had not given him the opportunity to do this. They, and that wife, therefore, had to be killed. The oldest brother and the second wife had to help. Thus, three family members are in jail for a long time; the four women are dead while three other children are left without any family. What a waste of human life!

A cultural belief like this goes a bit of a ways to explaining the use of the full burqa, which includes the facemask. Since it is not something I comprehend, it is hard for me to accept. I can see the covering of the hair. Being nearly bald and grey, I am not worried about having any man physically aroused and sexually attacking me, although I can see that a young man could really appreciate the gorgeous tresses of some of the girls today. I'm just thankful that I don't have to spend time looking after it. There is no such thing as a bad hair day, if you choose to have a covering. However, many of us, although we had no burqas, are still stuck with these invisible burqa rules of their culture. Honoring the father of the family was certainly one! My father was raised to believe that the full responsibility for his family was on his shoulders. He used to take me for walks and make sure that I stood straight, and did not point my toes in! This was the least of his instructions to me. My mother "toed the line" as well, and considered herself to be fortunate to have such a good, traditional husband.

That rule worked well in our homes until World War II was declared and the men were sent away. Suddenly my mother had the full responsibility. Did she ever enjoy it? His paycheck was given partly to him, but mostly to her for the family. She was the better financial manager, and by the end of the war, she was able to show him what she had saved. He saw the nest egg and immediately had designs on how to spend it. Needless to say, as with many returning soldiers, adjustments had to be made!

Fortunately, for us children, they did work out that problem. Mother won the money discussions—thank goodness. She was symbolic of many of the changes which then happened in society. The men had to regain their places. In some cases, there was no man, or the man was so damaged by what he'd endured, that it was impossible for him to adjust to family life here. The adjustment trauma that we are seeing with the returnees from Afghanistan is now at least recognized, and some help is available. Pity the thousands of veterans who had no help as they returned from the first two wars. Many became alcoholics, or died soon after their return.

In my generation, the women did promise to "*obey.*" It was part of the usual ceremony in most of the churches. The bride agreed to do what he said, and the groom promised to look after her in all of life's circumstances . . . "Till death do us part."

I was uncomfortable with that word, "obey", but was assured that my husband was a good man and it would not be a problem. In addition, my father told me that I must never be of the opinion that I had the right to change my husband in any way. I was to consider that I was a very lucky lady to have such a fine man. My mother added also that I was most fortunate. She just "knew" that he would be financially successful, and I would have a good life. This was from a woman who had to struggle all her life because she married a man who had grown up with money, and who had no idea of its purchasing power!

In most cases, if wives my age had jobs, they had to be jobs that were easily left. The women were expected to drop everything and move when the husband had a work transfer. I did that too. I was luckier than most as I was a teacher. At that time, I could usually get at least a substitute position. Then one could gradually work into a permanent placement. The fact that I taught for 30 years was really a bother to my mother. She kept asking me why I worked. She'd say, "Isn't he making enough money so you can stop?" I couldn't convince her that I loved being a teacher.

One real difficulty was that we'd all been raised to believe it was a rule that the mother must be in the home with her child or children. Her place was there while the father was at work. It didn't matter whether or not she found the days long and boring, once the last child was at school, and she had no car. Supposedly, she was the only one who knew what her child needed to become happy and healthy. Any mother who is stuck in the house with a crying first baby is bound to doubt that ability; it is rough. I had, at least, friendly and helpful neighbours. Once, my baby, who was less than three months, was screaming, and I had no milk. I'd been told never to let her have anything but the breast. I was sure she'd die. We were in a town house and a neighbor heard the cries and came with a full bottle of formula. I still believe she saved the infant's life. I could solve the problems of Grade 9 boys. I couldn't save my baby. I am sure that I am not the only mother to experience that terror. I envied my husband at work. Hillary Clinton is correct "It takes a village, as well as the parents to raise a child."

Ideas of family structure have changed a lot in my seventy-five years. Both mother and father expect to be recognized as individuals with their own ambitions, careers, and desires. Most parents realize that if they plan to have children, the children must come first, especially their needs, nourishment, and protection. Beyond that, each person should expect respect when each tell of their own ideas and wants. This concept was new to me. I had thought that it was still all about the saying, "You decide and I abide." We have both had adjustments to make since I realized that freedom!

Male and female genes really are different. For a partnership to work well, it does require: talking, and compromise, and compassion, and lots and lots of LOVE.

You Must Never Get a Divorce

T his was the way it used to be, and the way some people believe it is today. I beg you here to use your own thinking, and common sense. Does this marriage you are in really make your life worth living? "No divorce" has been the strict law in some churches for generations. Once you were divorced, you could no longer be considered a member of the congregation and could not take communion. Hence, you were going to hell. I am advocating that you do give your marriage: a good effort, lots of love, compromise, communication, and help if it is needed. Yet, there are times when all of these is not feasible and the situation is impossible to maintain. If so, then get a divorce!

The churches liked their control, and they got this by instilling fear. Such institutions wonder now why they are not popular, and why so many young people choose to live together, rather than being united by a service in a church. The problem now is that in our society people have been taught to think, and to question. It is harder now for churches to dictate to their members?

One of my very closest friends, whom I have known since high school, ran into this problem. She married her handsome heartthrob and moved from Toronto to live in the western United States. They were happy and he had a good job. They had children, a good home and she even had the chance to pursue her chosen occupation. It all looked so good . . . then it all fell apart. He decided not to work and problems piled on top of problems. He lost interest in his family. What choice did she have? She could not support her babies as well as him!

She piled them all onto the train and headed to Toronto. Her parents were in an apartment and helped her to get established in a place of her own. She got a job as a secretary with a good firm and proceeded to support her brood. Life was "ok" and the husband was never heard of again. Wouldn't you have insisted on a divorce? Those children were raised with lots of love and discipline. They are all now married happily, have good jobs and some even now have grandchildren. My friend is a great-grandmother. She is included in all their family celebrations, is much loved and is the venerated matriarch of the clan. What a loss for that father because he couldn't face his responsibilities!

When she needed the support of her church, she attended and was told by the minister that she was not welcome as she was a divorcee. She never went back. We have talked about this since and I have assured her that she would now be accepted because that particular idea has not been enforced for quite a while. She did go to other churches and try them. Unfortunately, she found that the ones she went to were most unfriendly. She even went to the coffee hours. It was no better! Then churches wonder why their numbers are shrinking! Daily Bible reading and perhaps a try at a different congregation appear to be the solutions, but the familiarity of the old service in which she was raised is missing. That matters at our age.

This is not the only friend of whom divorce was the better option. I'm not referring to women alone. The problems that arise afflict both sexes.

Another divorced friend says that men are all cut from the same cloth. It has 'me" and 'sex" printed all over it. The male patterns may be different, but the fabric is identical. Some of the women I know are from that material as well. A home with emotional divisions and upheavals is neither healthy for children, nor for the parents.

I firmly believe that the first years of married life require the most difficult adjustments. People can change if the will to change is there. Be sure to do your best to see each other's ideas and needs. There, I've removed the excuses people use when they say things such as: we just grew apart, or I never really knew him/her, or he/she expects me to change and I can't. If you are childless, then what is the problem? Are you fighting over material possessions or an animal? That is what lawyers are for; just don't let them take all that the two of you have accumulated. Remember you have a God-given right to make the best you can of your *one* life. If you need to have a divorce to do that, go for it.

BUT! Every baby in the world deserves to experience a secure and loving home for at least the first years of his/her life. The idea now is that this security is essential for development of confidence, hence success in later life. It was difficult, but my divorced friend accomplished this task alone. Those children would not have had the feeling of security if she had stayed in her marriage. We recently heard of an arrangement where, although the parents no longer love each, the parenting is shared by the dad living on the premises. Another couple have a shared parenting arrangement live apart, cut their places are close to each other. It must be hard, but the child knows both of them wanted her.

When people agree to set up a home, and even get married, most of us do not anticipate problems. We plan to make as happy and loving a home as possible. Problems can come from many sources. If there is sexual, physical, mental, or emotional abuse, the effort to save the situation becomes much more difficult. This is where professional help really should be tried. If it fails, probably reluctantly, you'll need to get a divorce or at least a legal separation.

If you have had a divorce, should you try to have a loving relationship again? That would not be easy and would require a lot of courage. Many young couples we know are doing this. They usually don't bother with the ceremony. That would take even more courage! We wish them luck and God speed as I know in my heart that the best way to live and to grow old is with someone you truly love and care about.

Rule 11

You Must Have Children

If you don't think this is a rule of life, just try listening to people in my generation; the ones who have been married, or who have partners, and now have grownup children. Far too often we hear these sad refrains: "We don't know when they will start a family, but we keep hoping." or "We have given up hope. Tell us what your grandchildren are doing." or "since the divorce, or the big move, we are only allowed to see them twice a year." These comments raise all kinds of questions. Did they really believe that their offspring would move in next door? Did they plan to spend the rest of their lives raising their child's children? Did they take the rejection of the idea of children as a personal insult? Are they wondering if they did such a bad job raising their child that their offspring would not want to be parents? If it is guilt, do they hope for a second chance to prove they are now better at parenting?

Grandparents who have their grandchildren living close are indeed fortunate; mine are in England. That is life! I felt that once my daughter was "launched" she had the right to make her own decisions. I'm happy for her independence. She seems as content, and as busy as she is supposed to be at her stage of life.

I have no illusions as I gladly live my own life, and they have their very own active and satisfying lives. In the meantime, my husband and I are lucky enough to have sufficient good health to travel where and when we wish. That would have been impossible, should we have had the added responsibility of grandchild care. If there were such a necessity, we would have done it. Yet, when our joints creak as we get out of bed each day, we thank God that wasn't' t in the cards.

Therefore, the decision about the birth of a child belongs solely to the people who would have the baby. How I wish we could provide sufficient birth control and education to any culture in the world where the daughters are raised to believe that they exist only to procreate. There are places where women are required to have as many children as possible, or where wives are "purchased" to have the babies, and to do the housework until the older woman dies. They, then are expected to live and take over the running of the large family. It's not only these girls who must reproduce. Would you like to be the Duchess of Cambridge? No! I trust that with the increased communication, especially TV, throughout the world, the lives of these girls will improve. However, it will not be in my lifetime—I suspect.

I do still believe that the world is getting better for both sexes. I get fed up with some people who are my age. I hear them repeat what I remember my own grandparents saying, "The whole of civilization is doomed!" Yes, there were wars then and there are wars now. Remember, we know that there will always be wars and rumours of wars, so if there is conflict, we should not have children! Wrong, our hope for the improvement of the world is in the wanted and planned children.

We hear of too many places in our world where the common method of birth control is abortion. The women who are "loving" people, and have already had as many children as they can feed are resorting to it. I can't imagine what I would have done had I been in China and the government had told me I could not keep my baby and had to have abortion. There are some special cases in our society when abortion is the right solution. It would not have been so for me. Sometimes the unwed mother is desperate and it truly is what is right for her. I think of the time I was approached by a Grade 12 boy and he asked if I would cover for his absence the next day. I agreed only after he explained. His girlfriend was pregnant and they could not be married. He wanted to go with the girl he loved to the clinic. I'd heard of many women who had to go through the procedure alone, and that must be hell.

One particular situation I want to tell about. There is a woman I met in jail, and she has been in the paper recently as she was arrested again for illegally picketing abortion clinics. This is her mission because her mother had been raped and had kept her baby, thus this woman has a life, which she treasures. Is she saving the babies? She is not. I was working in jail when she'd be there with the women I was teaching; she created havoc. The girls worked the streets and had had many abortions. They had very little choice as they had to get back out to earn money to support their drug habits. They'd arrive in our classroom in tears; she had undone the work we had done convincing them that they were loved and respected people who were capable of change.

Therefore, if you have the stamina and desire to raise children, God bless and help you. By the end of your life, if your offspring have had reasonably successful lives, had jobs and paid their taxes, you must believe that you have done your share to improve this earth. Pat yourself on the back. In fact, if they have contributed anything extra, that is a real bonus.

If you are still reading, it must mean that you are planning to, or have had children. Hopefully, they were planned and desired, or should it have been a 'slip", I trust that you have now fallen in love with that gorgeous baby. I'm serious when I say "fallen in love." I am serious. It was like nothing I'd never felt. Remember that, because when the child becomes a teenager, you'll need that memory! My friends who have adopted children have told me that it was the same love with their babies. Maybe it is even more so as those babies were so long anticipated. It was "a wait" that seemed worse than our usual nine months. I am glad that most women in Canada are now able to take the year from work for the bonding of mother and child.

Did you know that the fathers in Sweden are allowed to have additional time when the mother goes back to work? They can take up to six months, although I understand that not many do.

This parental bonding has now become recognized as one of the most important influences in the formation of the child's personality and overall growth. It is where his/her sense of self and confidence comes from. If you use childcare, make the weekends and evenings child centred. Leave the housework and meals to the minimum, or pay to have those jobs done . . . if possible. For many mothers this is all a pipe dream. I know that my niece in the United States, who is a professional, was able to take off only six weeks. She considered herself lucky! In some cases, a woman has to keep her job for the family's financial support; then there is just no choice. Whether or not mothers should ever work depends on too many variables to discuss here.

Concerning the proper way to raise your child, I haven't got a clue! The only thing I do know is that anyone who has a child, had a child, or will have a child is full of advice for you. Try not to listen. That is hard when that person is your mother, sister, or the neighbor of whom you depend for help with babysitting! The trouble is they all mean well, and want you to follow their advice in order to confirm that they are smart, and that they did a great job with their own offspring. You'll find this is true, even when you can see that their child is a mess! I've talked to mothers whose children were in jail. They still believe he/she only made a few mistakes, or it was the friends, not him/her, or that he/she just stood there and did not do anything. Such is any mother's (or father's) love that it is often impossible to realize that her child could have made a serious mistake.

Please remember also, that each child must be treated as an individual. They are all so different and it is hard to believe that all three of my grandchildren came out of the same gene pool. One often hears the comment, "I raised him just the way I raised his big brother or sister." No, you didn't! That child reacted differently to your consistent approach, whatever it was. One mother told me that if she raised her voice, her first daughter eventually did what she asked, but when the second heard a raised voice, she had to go look for the child under the beds. He needed only a whispered "please." Your tactics also have to be adjusted to the age and the developmental stage of the child. What one four-year-old accepts as a correction, another may regard only as a hurt, or a rejection.

I cannot even begin to realize the challenges of parents who have children with problems. In our family we have those with autism, down's syndrome, dyslexia, and dyspraxia. I had the latter two afflictions, and I know how hard and long my mother had to work with me so I could read, spell, and do adding.

If one is not having a child for love, then why? Historically most cultures simply regarded offspring as assets. In hunting, or subsistence farming societies, the more big healthy sons you have, the richer you are. Remember the opening scene of the TV show *"The Cartwright's?"* The wise old father comes riding home to his big house flanked by his three wonderful, powerful sons. Even today, some fathers still want that first baby to be a perfect son. Unfortunately, we hear today about female infanticide. We think it does not happen in North America. Yet, papers report that it does!

I remember reading once that in the olden days most of us felt the need to be assured that there will be someone to look after us in our old age. Is it a good reason to have a child? Pity my daughter. There are two of us and only one of her! The article told about how, in a Far East country, it was necessary to have at least eight babies to assure old age security. At least two would die before reaching the age of two. Half of those who are left would be girls and they'd get married and go look after their husband's parents. Of the three boys who remained alive, at least two would die before the last parent. Then one boy was left to support him.

Single mothers who make the decision to have a child cause some people to shake their heads. A few working women are now choosing that instead of never having a child. I think it is their right, and if they are supported by a loving family and have good jobs, why not? It is better than having a father who doesn't want a baby around. Some of the older women in jail really wanted a baby so they'd have someone to love and who would hopefully love them. However, they were realistic and realized the horror of trying to raise a child properly with so little money. How did they know? Often it was because they also had been raised by street mothers.

There are also parents who regard their children as necessary for carrying on the family traditions and heritage. I've done some research into my father's ancestors; it is fascinating to me. Why would I believe it was something everyone wants to know? I was excited when one of my cousin's granddaughters asked to talk to me about it. That was one descendent of how many offspring I can't even guess. My father's family had had nine children. Other friends I know have grandchildren so that the money they have worked so hard to accumulate will not go outside "the family."

Each person is entitled to her/his own ideas, and desires for progeny.

If you are still reading, and if you are a very wise, and a very loving person, maybe you should have children. As you've read by now, you know I had only one girl. We wanted more but couldn't. We were refused for an adoption. We were told we were too old; we were in our thirties! I guess that rejection made me a more loving and aware teacher. As with all people one meets, I found that every student had at least one character trait I could appreciate, and that made him/her at least a tiny bit loveable.

As I said, you will feel totally "in love", although scared, when you hold your first baby. Those feelings are normal. Relax . . . Yeah, right! You are indeed blessed if you have friends and family around who can give you supportive, but non-critical help. If not, ditch them! Seek out professional advice. There will be rough times. It is all part of the picture, all part of being really alive. You will learn the true meaning of <u>LOVE</u>. You will have learned and practiced the art of loving; sometimes even loving the unlovable. This is the kind of love which God has for us. This should be practiced on all the people you meet. It is so difficult. We all need it. Remember, the love you give to others comes back tenfold. It has with our child.

Rule 12

You Must Always Be the Martyr

If I hear, "Oh no, you go first." One more time, I really will yell at the person who says it. I feel maybe it is said to make me feel guilty for some reason. Which of the previous rules did I break? Was it my bad behavior? Did I fail to take turns properly? Do I have bad breath? Did I give the impression that I felt so superior that he/she had to bend to me? The end result, of course, is I try much harder to be "good" to that person, but in the end avoid his/her company.

Why do I react so strongly? I guess I have to solve that problem before I can examine the issue further. I know I really don't like playing the role of the "superior person." Why? I can do it if I have to, as evidenced by the fact that I was successful as a teacher. Maybe I'm just tired of it, but I don't think so. I enjoyed my job, and I acted as a boss because I believed that was effective classroom management. Now that I'm retired, do I still want to do it? Not really, but perhaps I do appear to act, speak, or have an imposing presence that projects a feeling of superiority.

I want my friends to consider me as on the same wavelength as they are, so we are able to share ideas and activities equally. If I think they might need help, I will ask them. I do expect real friends to reciprocate, if I need help. I don't want to be bossed around, and vice versa. I have friends who like to be in charge. I limit my time with them. I guess it's an ostrich approach, but it works. There are people who like all that guidance, and don't balk. Are they lazy, or lacking in initiative? I think they are martyrs, who are acknowledging someone else's right to have superior authoritative powers over them.

What does being a martyr mean, and what is the incentive to be one? The word comes from the idea which has been perpetuated by religions. Remember, we've been told stories of Jesus washing the feet of the disciples. If you don't wait on other people, and don't want to do good deeds for them, then you are considered to be a poor "believer" in many religions. Didn't religious figures like Jesus and Mohammad tell you to love and help other people? The people, who use this interpretation, seem to me to be forgetting the last part of the idea. They forget that Jesus said to love others, as much as you love yourself. That means you can't really care for others, if you are putting yourself down by acting humble, and are resentfully taking the role of the servant.

I have a story of a girl I'll call Helen. She lives in the country, and I heard about her from relatives who worry about Helen. In the same breath, they insisted she is doing what is right. She is self-supporting and works hard, hard enough to be able to rent a comfortable little home, of which she is very fond. She felt sorry for a neighbour, and did what she could to help her. That woman, Alice, was not poor, and owned her home. She was the perfect example of the hoarder that we have seen on TV.

The result was as one would expect. Alice's house burned so much that she could not live in it. I'm sure you can guess the rest of the story. That's correct. Helen let Alice move into her house. Now Alice expects Helen to feed her, and do her washing. She refuses to move! Would you move out if you were in Alice's comfortable position? Move, if you had it "that good"? They are both still in the house Helen rents. Helen works hard, and continues to look after her "visitor." Is Helen a martyr? Yes! Is she loving herself? No!

Are you obliged to support those who chose to lean on you, and chose not to look after themselves? That is the horror of being a martyr. Is that what you want to accomplish in life? It is a different story, of course, if you love the person, or are related and feel a familial obligation. My husband and I would do it for each other. That is a given. Do you sometimes question your actions? Is the person in need, or just a "leaner"? Are you being used? Couldn't you have been more help if you had shown her/him how to become self-supporting, and emotionally healthier?

Modern psychology seems to have awakened to this "new" concept. You aren't honestly helping if, in the back of your mind, you are resenting giving that help. Do you believe that they wouldn't even think of helping you? Is the help genuinely appreciated? Perhaps, you are just doing whatever caring thing you do with the hope that God is watching, and will let you in to His heaven! Worse still would be, if you are helping because you think those who hear of your good deeds will like you better. Forget that! It doesn't work. If they think of your actions at all, it will be that you were a fool because the ones you helped didn't appreciate it.

A difficulty of resisting the temptation to be a martyr is, as we now know, that to truly help people, you frequently have to be hard to be kind. The expression used now is that you are more helpful to teach a man to actually do the work of fishing, rather than to give him a fish. Also, we are hearing of "tough love" in relation to handling the problems created by a teenager. Many parents have had to say to a daughter, or son, at the age of sixteen, "If you plan to do that, and plan not to live by our rules, then you don't live in this house."

Helping people when your heart is not in it is for dire emergencies. What do you need to change? You need to learn to love yourself! Jesus's admonition is correct, however, I was raised that thinking of myself first was wrong. It was considered being selfish, a major sin. I'm sure many a young person went to confession, or said prayers, with this "being selfish" their only sin. (Later, of course, they would have more sins that are interesting!)

Was it so wrong to teach children to share, and to think of others? No. The proviso is that the parent should work on the "helping others" idea, at the same time as he/she instils in the offspring the idea that the child is unique and very much loved. The parent teaches a child to think that he/she is worthless, and raises that child who will never share or never help anyone. When you get to know the person who only thinks of herself/himself first, you will know that that person has not had a parent who taught him or her that he/she was worthy of love. Are you a person who thinks only of himself/herself? That is a "heavy" question. Can you be honest in your answer?

If you are ever going to learn to love yourself, you must also stop criticizing yourself. When you go to do something, do you hear a critical parent's voice in your ear? It doesn't matter if that parent is long dead. If you were told as a child that you were stupid, it is hard not to think all your life that you have that problem. Children who were negatively compared to siblings will suffer. If they were told that the big brother, for example, was better at sports; they will always feel that it is no use to try any sport. If it was reinforced by nagging and constant criticism, the idea will stick even longer. There will be more comments on how to learn to love yourself in the next few sections.

Try not to be a martyr just because you believe it will please a person who had a lot of influence in your life. I know of one man of whom financial success was his mother's way of valuing her children. His older brother was educated and successful. He, therefore, gave up on his personal life, worked hard, and became very rich. His mother was proud. Later, when he realized what he'd missed, he adopted a readymade family who had no father. He still, to this day, wants proof that they really love him. No matter how often they say it, he questions it. They love him so much, and try to make him feel included as much as possible in their lives. His wife, daughter, and grandchildren all adore him. They really do care.

One lady I knew by sight had been a martyr to her husband's every whim. She had given up her career to make sure he was successful in his—he is. I see his name in the newspaper. Did he stay with her? No! She said she had seen the woman he had chosen to replace her, and that she wasn't nearly as good looking. Was that a reason for her to lose him? I would guess that he wanted a partner who was his equal, and who loved herself enough not to be a martyr. There are many women who don't realize that their husbands are reacting negatively to the annoying "servant mentality."

One of my best friends loved herself enough to react positively after her husband left. She took a good job. She went back to school. She made a great success of her international career. She had self-confidence. She loved herself enough because when she was growing up there had been lots of love from her parents and grandmother. Did he come back? Yes.

Although the martyr syndrome is more prevalent in women, men can exhibit these behaviors. Some of the old courtesies men were expected to show to ladies should be questioned. They would act as though they worshipped the lady. Did they really? Were those moves used to get the woman into bed? Whom did they really want to help? Were those men really belittling themselves and being martyrs, or was it a devious self-serving behavior? I know of a mother who actually made a martyr of her son. He was made to feel it was his obligation to stay with her, and look after her in her old age. He never even married, or had a girlfriend she knew about!

If you truly love yourself, do you question every kindness you receive? No! Learning to accept graciously is proof that you are on the way to believing that you deserve such treatment. Every time you smile and you say, "Thanks," you are telling yourself that you are a good person, and deserve the care of your fellow humans. Call that "thanks" an ego booster, or whatever you wish, but it does help you learn to love yourself. Hence, the more you give help gratuitously, the more thanks you receive, the more boosts your ego gets; then the more you love yourself. Love is definitely a circular force.

Self-love will not happen immediately. Stop doing caring things just to get approval, especially if you are feeling like a servant. Remember to do those good deeds because you know it will make another person feel better, and maybe even be happier.

Look around you. Open your eyes to the need and the misery. Ask yourself, what could I do to help? It may be very little, just an appreciation that the person smiled at you and you could smile back. You might even risk weird public looks and smile first. Never miss a chance to give a compliment; we all need them. The media images and the traditional methods of raising children can lead to developing a real lack of self-confidence. Also, you might be able to help in another way. If you have the resources to make a difference with money, do it. It could mean such a lot to the recipient; you may never know how much. Actions really do speak much louder than any words, but the words are a start in your quest for your own self-confidence and self-love. Remember, it is okay to love yourself.

I know I just implied that you will be warmed by thanks. Let me assure you that if you give any kind word, or action without a thought of gratitude being expressed, it is a better feeling. Now, if you are not even known to the receiver, it is the best feeling of all. You can't help loving yourself! Your future kind actions will not be done with hope of return or profuse "thanks"; they will be done for your inner "feel good" self-love. You will have stopped being a martyr. Try it!

You Must Let Others Control Your Life

There are people who hope to justify their own existence by improving your life. This applies firstly to parents who usually think that it is their responsibility, even if you have grown up and left home. Maybe they wish to see you achieve the goals, which they never did. Most of my ancestors had been teachers, and I was expected to become one. My father even said that I was so bossy that it was the job at which I'd be successful. I was. I had really wanted to try social work and couldn't afford the tuition when the time came, and I had fallen in love. I did have the required degrees to be qualified to teach. As with most teachers, my first year was hell, but after more experience, I realized that my father had been right that teaching was the correct profession for me.

Many other "older" people may also believe they should give you advice, advice that is often not in your best interests, nor to your benefit. They may even suggest ideas that are to their benefit, not yours. I think of the girls in Russia who were told that they would have a good life if they went to Europe for different and better paying jobs. They'd be told just to get in touch with a certain man; he would have waitress jobs for them. I've seen them on the side of the roads in France hoping that the truck drivers will stop so they could "turn a trick or two." The "man" would be standing behind them, hidden in the trees, making sure they never kept any of the money they received.

Usually, however, the advice from others is well intended, such as when a mother nags at the daughter to lose weight, or curl her hair so that the boys will ask her on dates more often. The more this was said, the more the situation worsened for most of us. Although done "out of love," that advice is counterproductive and hurtful. It caused me to be defiant and sneak food. "I'm only thinking of your happiness." That was the remark that usually followed such advice. Generally speaking, most of us had not been given enough self-confidence to talk back, and say bluntly, "shut up!' We'd been told to respect our elders. It was one of the cardinal rules of getting along with people. I used to wonder why the older people did not have to respect me. Think about it. How many times have you considered the point of view of a child, when you thought you had the right to correct him/her? Did you later apologize? You should have.

There has been much written lately in the media about the rearing of children. The "experts" believe that your guidance will be more effective when you meet the children at their level. Listen, and try to understand their thinking. It is also important that they understand your reasoning too. Don't give in to them. Children often can't see the whole picture. Don't be too lenient. The "little monsters" can be very self-centered, and do have to be shown how to be compassionate, and have to learn that they should respect the rights and feelings of others if they are going to survive in this "cruel world." I recognize that this is particularly difficult should the little one be handicapped in any way. So now that I've given you my "expert advice" of children. Whose advice should you be wary of?

Friends and neighbors are very often free with help and with talk, more free than you may wish. This is so true concerning help with children. Yet, there are times when it can be essential. My daughter might have died without my neighbour appearing with that full bottle of formula. It is also hard to remember that your free "advice" might be considered as interference instead of help. Information such as, "Well, my baby walked much earlier than your baby." That comment can be extremely hurtful. No mother can control the rate at which her child progresses through life. Such "free" comparisons are difficult for any parent to accept because we all believe that our baby is the "top of the class."

Many of us don't have self-confidence, or are too shy to ask for help. It takes belief in yourself to accept that you may need advice. Learning to love yourself does help here. Then you can realize that others might have some things to teach you, because you do know that you have things to teach them based on your own life experiences. You'll be surprised to discover people will have assistance to offer you if you have the confidence to ask them. It might even be a mutual exchange. I've found that at my advanced age, women will ask things such as, "What should I do about my child? She/he is getting a divorce." I think that the best answer I can give is, "You be there when that person wishes to talk, and then be prepared to listen." This works best. Try to give the troubled person the confidence that he/she will do what is right for them. First, always ask for their own solutions, and ideas. They may already have the best ones, and just want them confirmed!

Doing your own thinking, and making your own decisions are essential; it is your life! It is hardest to prepare children for these skills, which are so essential for their teen years. Their friends are in their faces, and social pressure is very real and the freedom is attractive. I know about it as I buy the requisite brand of t-shirts for my grandsons. Am I giving in to peer pressure? You bet. Am I a bad grandmother? I hope not. I justify it by saying that I am teaching them that such things in life are not life threatening; it doesn't hurt to listen occasionally. I am fully aware that the clothing does make a teenage boy have a little more confidence. The "right" shirt means he will not be mocked. Other teenagers can be extremely cruel. Teenage years are difficult as one tries so hard to gain self-confidence, to learn that other people don't always know best, and to make the right decisions.

When I'm asked for advice I try to follow the idea that I'm alive to love God, myself, and others. What if I can see that my advice could help? I have done a degree in psychology, and been trained as a school guidance counsellor. My family believe I should stay out of other people's lives. They believe in "live and let live." I believe, though, I have averted a few crises, but in my old age, I learned a few things too. Most people have thought through their own problems. If I'm approached, I ask, then really ask again and again. If they persist in having no answers, then I ask about solutions they might not have thought of. Most, however, do only want to be confirmed in their ideas and their own solutions.

Follow the advice of others only if you decide it is right for you. Think of the people who will be affected by your actions. Do the least harm to the others. Remember . . . love yourself. Then you are ready to love and help other people.

One of my soul mates died recently. It was a "good" death, and I was able to tell her friends and family that at her memorial service. It is not too often that one meets a person whom you can call a "soul mate." The more we talked, the closer we became. Mainly we talked about the major trials we had had in our relatively long lives. There were a lot of similarities in our family homes, and in the parenting ideas of our mothers and fathers. These concerned the rules I'm discussing in *The Invisible Burqa*: rules that thankfully really have changed a lot today. If all this writing ever amounts to anything, I will dedicate it to my friend, Mary.

For most of her life, Mary's actions and her speech were dictated by what she believed was expected of her. When her parents were around, she was as perfect as they expected. She was the only daughter and had six brothers. When she and her mother went on overnight visits to a favourite aunt, she slept with a female cousin who was the same age. The cousin would pinch her, and she didn't dare to tell. She believed what she had been told, her own mother would have been seen in the family as not having control of her child. She already knew that suffering in silence was expected of her.

Hence, there was a wall, and no communication with the one person whom she needed. Once when she was about ten or eleven, she saw her mother sobbing and was scared to offer a hug. She wanted to, but felt it would be misunderstood, and she'd be punished. She couldn't even tell her mother about the priest who sexually abused her. Abuse which started when she was a child and continued until she was a teenager. He was the one whom her mother trusted. My own mother was equally sensitive to the judgement of her family. When I was quite young, I overheard her repeat to a neighbor the feelings which I thought I'd told her in confidence. That was the end of my trust and my confidence at home.

Mary obviously didn't let her mother know all about her feelings and the things she and her brothers did. She told me, for example, of the fun they had at the *CNE* after they went in by going over the fences, or under! She was very close to the brothers who were nearer her own age, especially the only one who was younger. She regarded herself as a mentor for him and his friends and cousins. They adored her. At her memorial service for, her brother told about how she had made his graduation night important and memorable, by loaning him the car she had worked for so hard. Many people had similar stories of her caring for and about them. Mary hated school, particularly Math class. As a result, her graduation was in the commercial subjects, and she felt she was a failure. She then went to work in offices. She didn't really hate it, but it was not what she liked especially. She enjoyed the money, had the car and many friends. She was popular and pretty.

Pressure to get married came from home. She took a look at her mother's difficult life, and said, "No." In spite of the abuse by the priest, she decided to be a nun. As the family drove her to the initial place for training, her mother begged her all the way there to reconsider. She wanted Mary to get married, and seeing the hell of her mother's life, resisted.

It was a very strict order which she joined. Mary wanted so much to have a life in which she felt useful to other people, and had hoped that by joining she could become a nursing sister. The mother superior refused the request. It was not to be, as Mary had office skills. She could be put to work immediately in the office where they had a need for her. The principle, of course, was that she was there to serve God, so He wanted her to be doing office work.

The next idea that she found repulsive was that she was innately a sinner. That was so difficult because she did have a true sense of right and wrong, and had always tried to listen to that inner voice. Some of the sins they talked about she'd never even known existed! She was taught self-flagellation, given her own knotted cord, and told to practice it regularly. I was horrified as I'd thought that that idea went out with the Dark Ages.

The last straw was the scolding she got the night that she befriended a street person. She had let him sit in the hospital lobby, and had even offered him coffee. The weather outside was a snowstorm, and he had asked for shelter. She left her order with nothing . . . not even the suitcase that Maria was carrying in *The Sound of Music*! Then her mother turned against her. She was told she had let God down, and was a sinner.

As you can imagine, the resulting mental struggle was huge. Fortunately, the health care system became involved. Mary met very wonderful and very helpful people. She recovered with their help and by her own knowledge that what she was doing was right for her. She devoted her life to being a help to all of her friends and acquaintances, and to learning as much as she could. It had been a terrible blow to be told that she was too "stupid" to be a nurse. She took courses and succeeded at university level, and did some excellent writing. Unfortunately, at the end of her life, she decided to have all her writing destroyed. She felt some of it might offend her family. That was her choice. I had suggested that as an impersonal reader, I could sort it, but she decided it was too chancy. She didn't want, even then, to take a chance that anyone would be hurt.

I want to include her with the one poem that she did leave to her best friend, Rob. It was a "good" death as she knew at the end that Jesus was right. She had a right to be loved, and to love herself.

"Peace."

This is temporary
You are melting your tumor
Three puffs when possible.
Watch the smoke against the green hedge.
Remember the green drink.

Sometimes you'll need to rest.
Pay attention to what you need to eat
To what you don't want to eat. Don't force yourself to eat,

A minute at a time . . .
Enjoy what you love and appreciate.
Drink some Ensure.
Remember all the people who love you.
Appreciate just being alive!

Written by Mary

Rule 14

You Must Avoid Change

O f all the rules I have been discussing, this is the one which is most commonly accepted, and is regarded as being written in stone. It could even be considered the eleventh commandment. Many of us can think of a change we'd like to see in our lives, or environment, yet we lack the initiative, or maybe believe that we can't actually change. Life is so much easier when one stays in the comfortable, but acceptable, rut. BUT! Every new day brings changes.

One summer we rented a cottage in Cape Cod. We'd been there many years earlier and loved Dennis Port. Our daughter was now old enough to ride a bike, so we loaded the three bikes in a special rack built by my husband. It was a long drive from Toronto, but worth it. The cabin, which we had rented sight unseen, had to be cleaned before we could go to sleep. A couple who were in their eighties owned these buildings, and when we got to know them, we were so pleased we hadn't chosen to move. The owners were delightful and regaled us with stories of their sons, of whom they were properly proud. All of their sons were either doctors or scientists. One of them had won a Nobel Prize!

Later, we became acquainted with the people who owned a cottage behind ours. We asked if they'd met the owners of our cabin, and the answer was negative. What they had missed! My husband helped this new acquaintance, a lawyer, who was not too good with his hands. His wife, a teacher, had bought a shed that needed to be put together, and she couldn't do that alone. We got to know them quite well. The lady expressed amazement at the number of places we'd been, and the things we'd seen. She had been born in the State of Maine; and had made the big trip to the Boston area where she met and married her husband. He had grown up and been educated there. They had never left. Her fondest dream was to have a car trip to the White Mountains. We assured her the scenery there was wonderful.

She could not change her life and make this trip. I suggested that she might like to go without her husband, maybe on an organized bus tour. That change of being without the husband was just too scary. She couldn't believe that we would not be coming back to that same cabin next summer; that we planned to take a different holiday the following year!

We Canadians tend to act superior, and say that the Americans never travel; they do. We too are inclined not to change if we don't need to, and be too inclined to stay comfortably at home. Canadians, though, can change and move around if we must. Witness the trek of the Newfoundlanders to the Alberta Oil Sands for work. They are a people who will not be satisfied with "bogey," if there is a chance for a job. They know the comfortable and the known are attractive, but not at the cost of their self-esteem. How many of us need a bit more of the old "get-up-and-go"? Taking initiative requires a lot of self-confidence, and building that is what should be the chief aim of all education. This process begins in infancy. We are told that the baby, who is left alone unloved, will soon stop expecting any attention. This is because the infant learns to sooth him/herself and that he is not worthy of receiving love from an external source.

Why don't people have this attitude of being open to life's opportunities, challenges, and changes? The answer to the question is that it is easier and safer where they are. Probably, the reason is that the person who raised the child unconsciously instilled a lot of the need for security. If the adult dislikes bugs, thunder, or even the father, then the child learns by example to be wary of those sources of potential suffering.

Historically, we were programmed to be aware of dangers in order to survive. If you've read any of the books in *Clan of the Cave Bear* series, then you know what I'm mentioning. Our ancestors really did get eaten by "big" animals. Today people can even develop fear of little animals. Fear of such small things as bacteria is very real. This has been more logical recently as we have learned about how the germs have become more resistant to our various medicines. We even hear of the potential of germ warfare. Germs may be a quite logical reason to refuse to travel if you have the possibility of severe allergic reactions, and especially if there are no medicines, you might need, available in the country to which you wish to go.

Resistance to any changing of behaviour patterns can be taught by the parents, and by anyone else whom the child regards as an authority figure. Pain is an effective teacher. In the old days this was a common device of those who did not know how else to control classes. You may have heard of the whole class being lined up to get the strap from the teacher. It happened to me only once and by the time the teacher arrived at my hand she was too tired to really make me feel pain; I only felt anger.

Sometimes reaction of changing is the only smart response to a changing situation. During the Nazi occupation, a family I know were a part of the route for the Jews escaping from Germany. The children were told never, ever, to give any indication that some people were hidden in spaces under the grain bins. They obeyed well due to very reasonable threats. For health, it is also sometimes sensible to change behavior. My surgeon told me not to ski after I have my new knee. I put up arguments, but he was adamant. I argued that my friend who had had two knees replaced still went skiing. He still refused my permission. Lately, the girl was really scared when in a tricky position on a hill, and she had to get the ski patrol to take her down. I guess my doctor was right.

I used to be a timid person, afraid of physical challenges and social situations. I have changed. When thinking about trying to accomplish a feat you regard as difficult, hesitation is usually smart. Have I always obeyed the instinct? No. Do I regret that? . . . in only one or two cases! Yet, if I'd obeyed my "gut," think of the thrills and the fun I would have missed. In his older years, my father and I went on a rollercoaster. My mother did not. As was her wont, she lacked the courage. Daddy and I had such fun! In my favourite daydream I'm in the sunshine swishing gently down the perfect ski run in a perfect bowl at a high French mountain ski resort. I have done that. Don't let your life be ruled by physical challenges, but be prudent. Assess the risks, and balance them against the thrills. I would never ski "off piste" as my relatives do, but I did challenge myself sometimes! Try to die with as few regrets as possible.

Teens often refuse opportunities and suffer from the fear of accepting life's challenges. They realize something should be tried, but the courage is lacking. I can speak from experience. When one is maturing, he/she does regard the opinions of the peer group as terribly important, and I do mean "terribly." Such unkind remarks on the internet have caused teens to commit suicide. Now, we are right to regard these 'slings and arrows" as dangerous. Surviving attacks on self-confidence is extremely difficult. Often teens change behaviour, character, or appearance just to avoid the criticism of their peers; these are not always changes which would really make their lives better. Yet, to have stayed as they were would have engendered even more damaging gossip, and abuse.

I think that this is one of the hardest problems parents have to deal with today. How does one shield a child? Even as an old lady, I'm susceptible to what I call social fear. I cope by retreating from an uncomfortable scene. Since I am "relatively" confident now and have places to hide, I'm okay. Teens who have special areas of competence in life do seem to cope better. Maybe it will be in music, in sport, or in drama, or in just being the class clown. It helps if the ones who need help have been encouraged to talk to an adult whom they trust. Having at least one close friend is essential to building the confidence required when facing unrelenting criticism.

This threat of exposing a weakness can be real and almost impossible to deal with, if one has been encouraged to be shy, or if one carries a deep secret. Some children are taught that drinking in the home is shameful and they will never tell it to even one friend for fear that this secret will be public knowledge. Pity the child, who has been threatened with punishment, if he/she reveals the fact that he/she is being sexually abused.

Other influences exist which make a person to resist changes, changes which could have been beneficial to them. Other people could make you reconsider a change by their taunts and threats: "If you take the new job, then I will not move to live with you." There are also the religious threats of hell and severe punishment from the great and powerful, angry God in the sky. Are you going to give up that chance for a heaven, which is promised, by certain churches? Are you then giving up a chance for any happiness in your earthly life? I'm not, as my God is not like that. I can use the brain He gave me to decide what is right for me. If He is disappointed in me, I am very aware of it. I feel so guilty and so sorry. I know He knows my suffering, and knows that I'll try to do what is right the next time. My God forgives!

There was a horrible accident recently in which a young driver forgot to think about his actions, and he ignored the danger factor and chose the thrill factor instead. He figured he could drive at excessive speed while drunk. That big SUV was cut in half. It happened in Toronto, on Mount Pleasant Road, at 2:00 a.m. The disastrous results stopped the traffic for hours. He lived but his friend was killed. How will he live with that? It was certainly a very real change which a bit more use of "intelligent thought" should have prevented.

Now that I've scared you into inaction, what is to be gained by accepting change and life's challenges? Everything! It is what is meant by being alive. How else are discoveries made? How else are records set? How else are successful careers established? How else do you make your contribution? What will you want to be able to answer when you reach my age and people ask, "What do you regret?"

Look at all the friends and relatives whom you know well. Are they happy? Are they having satisfying and productive lives according to the rhythm of their own ideas and wishes? Are they merely content in their ruts? Which life do you want? Are you now a contributing member of society? Really, talk to those people whom you wish to emulate. Then, consider what works for them and of their ideas, choose which ones work for you.

Remember, you should regard your life as your own. Don't give anyone else its control. If you are not content, ask yourself why. Ask what changes you need to make, and if they can be done without causing pain for too many other people. Are family obligation, essential, or are you fostering unnecessary dependence which causes their failure to mature, or for them to stop taking the responsibility for themselves? Watch out for the guilt trips done by those who wish to control you for their own purposes. It does not matter what age you are. Maybe, for example, even a change in your health routines might increase the number of years you have in which to make a difference to the world, and improve your own happiness.

Really, ask yourself if you love yourself. If not, change! How do you expect to help and love others if you do not love yourself enough to make the changes to become alive?

Rule 15

You Must Have a Religious Affiliation

I t doesn't matter what belief system you have been raised in or have decided to adopt, this rule is usually used to persuade one to attend a service of worship regularly. In my lifetime, in the Christian religion, we had this ingrained when we were young. Any church member, if absent, could expect to hear, "Why weren't you at church yesterday? Were you ill?" (Or perhaps not in the temple, synagogue, and mosque or . . .). It is a pretty strong implication that you are not a good person, if you disobeyed this rule. Many people nowadays do not have any connection to any organization that is designed for religious observations.

I was not in church last Sunday! Why? I was in England and had a bad fall. So what was your excuse for not going to any place of worship recently? Was it: the beautiful weather? The trip you had to take? The work that had to be done for Monday? The dislike of the person who was speaking that day? Maybe even having fallen in England? I think I've used them all and more. I'm guilty. But . . . should we feel guilty? Does God really punish those who don't go, those who don't even pretend to go, or those who don't even pretend to want to belong to any group of fellow believers?

I do not believe He does. The God I have come to understand would much rather have you in a place where you feel His presence, instead of being in a place where all you can think of is how fast you can do your duty, and get out. I can't believe, either, that He wants you to attend out of fear. If you go because you're afraid of the condemnation of the other people, or worse still, the fear of hell when you die, then don't go. I think you might as well stay home, or better yet go for a good walk and admire nature, or be helpful to someone who needs your help. I'm convinced that is what Jesus would advise. Don't forget! He healed the sick on His Sabbath, and got into trouble with the "church people" of his day!

So, then why do I go? I'll try to explain it the best that I can, but I'm not trying to convince anyone that what I do is right for others. I think that the need and reasoning are very individual. I can only explain the thinking that I went through. I had been raised in the Anglican Communion and believed the entire dogma. As a family, it was routine to go to church each Sunday. Many of my thoughts, when there, were not necessarily very holy, especially as a teenager when I gazed at the handsome young men around me! This attendance at church was obligatory even for when I was at university as I lived at home and was not allowed to plead that I needed to work on the essay that was due.

Then I graduated, got a job away from home, and didn't go to church for a year. I didn't miss it; I considered myself a member of my old church. I was being married from that place of worship. Next, after marriage, we were in Montreal and the local buildings were all Catholic, so that was the excuse. When we moved to Toronto, we felt obliged and attended the Presbyterian Church of my husband's past, based in the idea that the husband leads! Now, we have agreed and have become members of a United Church. We both believed that it was necessary to give our child a foundation of religious teachings. When she was older and rebelled about Sunday school, she and I went to the basement to look after the babies.

The United Church we attend is the closest one to the philosophy to which I adhere at the present. I try to follow Jesus" dictum: "Love and honour God, and love your fellow human beings as much as you love yourself." The last bit of that is what most people ignore, or don't believe. You really do need to love yourself. There is nothing more disconcerting than to be helped by someone whom you sense is "looking down" on you. Does it feel as if they are only pretending compassion, but that they really feel superior? To be a giving person, you have to give love to yourself first!

There is a wonderful poster at the Dorothy Ley Palliative Care Centre that lists all the world's religion. It has a sentence beside each one that states its philosophy. It is in a room set aside for contemplation and mediation. In various ways, they all say we must love our God, and love and serve our fellow humans.

So then, why do we have all these religious wars? I think we fail to live in peace because we tend slavishly to follow the ideas, which "wise men" and "prophets" have written down for us. We have never learned to question, and to think, and to make our own life's decisions. We should question which ideas mean a lot to us, and which can be ignored. My sister scolded me severely when I suggested that I believed that Jesus had the "right" ideas, but that I'd question many of the sayings of Saint Paul which she accepted as true. When the Catholic scholars composed the New Testament, they used many of those writings to promote the concepts, which lead to control—control for their priests over the people.

Also, remember that much of our Christian part of the Bible was created centuries after Jesus lived. What He taught us about what God expected of us is in many different writings. Did you know that a large number of manuscripts about Jesus were recently found buried in Egypt? Remember the Dead Sea Scrolls. They were not discovered until after the New Testament was composed. We must learn to question what "wise" people say. God gave us the ability to think and the freedom to make our own decisions. This applies to the dicta of many religions. Do you believe that you must never kill the mosquito that is biting you? You would, if you were of the Buddhist faith.

Any religious institution that tells its member to change the belief systems of other people is wrong. God wants us to think for ourselves. Remember Jesus sat in the temple and questioned the leaders, and used His brain. At His trial and His crucifixion; He made it very clear that there was much to question about the beliefs and rules the Jewish leaders followed.

Why then, do I go fairly regularly to my church? Why do we contribute to it financially? I believe that many of our church's programmes do need my help, and I contribute time and money to those I think really helps people in need. My church sponsors: a food bank, a yearly clothing sale with prices for people who need clothes, struggling congregations in needy areas, AA and NA programmes, an active young people's programme across Canada, out-of-the-cold dinners, volunteers who do after school tutoring, and it provides real support each year for a different immigrant family. There are also probably some more "good deeds" which I don't even know about.

This is why I belong. As a bonus, I like the music and I love to sing! I also appreciate the chance to thank God for my many blessings. In the prayers and sermons, I get help to understand His will for me. Incidentally, the people whom I call my friends there are remarkable and loving fellow humans. Most have made far greater contributions to the world than I ever will. There is lots of God's LOVE and warmth in that congregation. I appreciate that feeling.

Have you found a place that can give you that contentment and LOVE? If not, why not start looking?

Rule 16

You Must Obey Religious Teachings

I am referring to the rules, which religious organizations, and society, have imposed on us for their control. We can't ignore the rules which we all had to learn as children to help us survive socially. We learned pretty quickly that if we hit our friends too often, then they would not play with us. Other similar ideas came soon. If we had been sent for a religious indoctrination as well, there would have been there additional rules to follow.

Laws which are for the benefit of all society are enforced by governments—rules from religious institutions are not. I believe that most monotheistic religions have similar structures for life, and for the spiritual health of their members. In my early church years, I had to memorize the Saint James Biblical version of the Ten Commandments, as well as other passages of the official catechism before I could be confirmed. We would then be confirmed by the visiting bishop and be allowed to take communion. We were told that taking regular communion was necessary for a happy afterlife.

As I have previously hinted, I no longer believe these religious laws were written by God's hand, and given as stone tablets to Moses. These rules did, I'm sure, prove to be a great help to Jewish leaders in controlling their people when they were wandering in the desert. During forty years, the people were increasing in number. Much of our legal system today is actually based on many of these concepts, as many of the ideas are still held to be true and important today.

As you have gathered from my preceding writing, I hold strongly to the idea of one God. There are many monotheistic religions. It seems logical to me that God must have revealed His LOVE to more than just one society. We all have differing rites, different requirements for the worship, and different ways of acknowledging one God. To me, He is the immense power of LOVE. People all over the world have felt and experienced it. That LOVE is obvious in their writings and philosophies. (If it turns out, as some believe, that He really is a revengeful old man in the clouds, I hope He has a sense of humour, and genuine forgiveness.) The concept of God is also in the works of those who protest so loudly that there is no God; they thus acknowledge His Presence when they believe they can blame Him for all the problems. They forget that His most significant gift to us was free will, our ability to control our own actions and their consequences!

The first commandment, which is to honour God and is also a ruling against worshipping "graven images", was appropriate for Moses" time. People apparently felt closer to a god if they could actually 'see"—so images were made. Remember the story of the competition of the prophet Jeremiah against the prophets of the god named, Baal. In that story, Jeremiah, with God's help, wins; then he uses the jawbone of a donkey to kill those "false" prophets!

I guess he forgot one of the later commandments! Today, one does not have to look too far to see how worship of "graven images", and/or material possessions, and these pursuits, cause one to lose sight of the most important thing in life, LOVE.

I suggest that the idea of honouring one's parents is open for questioning. Some mothers and fathers really do not deserve much respect. However, they are still our familial responsibility. Should help be required, we give it. Do so as willingly, and with as much love as you can muster. Try to see where they were coming from in their own lives. It does make it easier if you can at least feel compassion for any suffering they may have endured. The mother, who was a hopeless alcoholic, was perhaps raised by a mother who had the same sickness. Remember, one learns to be abusive from having been abused.

I honestly think that the next commandment in the list should be the admonition against being covetous, or in present day language, "jealous", and wanting what other people have. Isn't this the cause of gossip (bearing false witness)? Doesn't jealousy lead to hurting others, to stealing, to adultery, and to murder? Most of the laws we live by in our societies are based on the idea that it is wrong to want things we don't and can't have. This feeling gets in the way of our loving others. This desire to have more, even when we already have the rudiments of a comfortable life, can be explained by jealousy. Is it not why Ponzi schemes are so effective? Why do the wealthy, famous "one per cent" commit crimes? Why is it that the larger yacht is so obviously "needed", if not to make one's rich friends to covet and experience envy and feel jealousy?

In Toronto, we do have people who truly are in dire need. I've known and helped enough citizens who live on the margins, to realize some of our citizens do have very real struggles just to get by. I'm not stupid enough to say comments to annoy those living with illnesses, or those who are living with the regrets that they did not avail themselves of earlier opportunities. I heard a lot of inmates, for example, who truly regretted their choice to leave school early. I believe that our school system did not meet the needs of many students. Police and social workers in the schools are a necessity the government does not wish to finance. We definitely require many more social workers to help all people get help. A lot of assistance is available if one knows, or is shown, how to get it.

When I hear complaints that it would cost too much, I want to scream. There are many cases where a little help would save much money. If these people could be helped, they would become productive members of society. My particular protest is about the refusal of the various governments to fund education for inmates who have not yet been sentenced. Some of these people are even innocent, but they all just spend unconscionable amounts of time at great expense waiting for a trial. There is precious little or no rehabilitation during this wasted period.

Why do we expect citizens of the under developed world not to feel jealousy, and not to covet what we have in Canada? With worldwide TV and the internet, they must be totally aware of their deficiencies in goods and living conditions. Our help is totally inadequate.

This brings us to the biggest question of all, which I have about the Ten Commandments. The people of Israel were told that they were not to commit adultery. It meant there is sexual intercourse only allowed with a person to whom there is love and/or commitment. If you are only having sex with someone for fun, it was wrong, or for revenge, it was wrong. Butand it is a big "but", what if you really do love the person with a compassionate love, and have no real commitment to each other? What if, as well as your genuine love, there is also a certain magical, sexual tension? What do you do? Wiser people than I failed to answer that. It is truly up to you. Remember this decision is also about the other people who are involved in your lives who might be hurt. Should you be so lucky that you have no previous commitment to others, you decide. Just remember that babies are to be wished for; they are not "accidents."

I hear you. I hear you. You are wondering about the teaching of marriage first before sex. That is a personal decision, and not to be taken lightly. Are you old enough, really mature enough, to make the decision? Can you envision spending a lifetime with this person? Are you honestly prepared to support a baby? The questions keep coming. Only you can answer them for yourself. If you have other obligations, then I would not wish to make such decisions for you. I do not have to live with the results of your decisions. One comment though . . . Divorce is now morally and socially acceptable. I do not believe the God that I understand, who is LOVE, would want you to deny yourself His greatest gift of a committed, loving relationship with your soul mate. If making such a change in your life would hurt those around you, then it's your struggle. Could you hurt them? Could you live with yourself if you did? Be brave. Ask these special people for input to your decision. Maybe they'd be very hurt, but still want you to be fulfilled. That is the real love I'm talking about.

Ask God. How? Pray. I'll give you a very personal idea here. I do not go through a priest, or make suggestions to God during a church service. Find your own way to talk with God. This is what works for me. I find that I pray by being absolutely quiet, and in my very own space. I mentally present my question to God. I listen in the silence to hear a response. The answer often is not immediate. It can come when I least expect it. I'll give you an example. I may see a need for a special friend, or maybe a need for someone I don't know that well. I tell God I don't know how to be a help. Then, the next time I see him/her the answer will suddenly be so obvious.

In the Christian religion, we have a prayer, which we are told, Jesus gave us. I particularly like a version from one of the earliest

Christian writers. It was recorded long before our Biblical version. It is from a source of our Bible referred to as the "Q":

"Father, Your name is holy. Deliver us to your kingdom. Provide us with the bread we need each day. Forgive our debts, as we have forgiven those in debt to us."

Jesus is saying here that God knows our earthly needs, and will provide the food we need to sustain life. If we look after our bodies that he gave us, and live in peace with each other, then all we really need to ask for is to be with Him when we die. So . . . love God. Love yourself. Love and help others.

You Must Never Question
Beliefs from Childhood

These man-made beliefs will guide you all your days. They will guarantee your eventual entry into heaven where you will be in paradise. You will be able to look down on all the "friends" who, you know, broke these rules. They are the "wicked ones" who had all the fun, while you were being so good. Now, aren't you glad you had such a righteous, "boring" life?

No! No! No! What if you never grow up and learn to question what is right or wrong for you as a separate individual? Granted, there are many such manmade rules which work well for most people, and they should be considered seriously as you mature. At a certain stage of maturity, you have a God-given right to decide freely how you are going to act during your lifetime on earth. Remember, as you make these decisions, that your life may indeed be very short. You may not have many years in which you are able to "redeem" yourself, both in your own estimation, and in the estimation of those whose opinions matter to you (God?).

Most organized religious initiations have these lists of formalized "suggestions." One church I can think of says that you must never stand for the national anthem because that would be worshiping an idol. Personally, I decided to dismiss that idea long ago, as I'm very glad to live in Canada, and am proud of my country, and of its contributions to the welfare of the rest of the world. As for me, I really appreciate all Canada offers.

As I implied in "Rule 16," one should believe most parents when they tell you to follow their instructions regarding their tried and trusted ways of coping with the challenges of life. This is generally a wise move, and not hard to follow if you have been raised by people whom, you know, really loved you. If you believe they made some mistakes along the way, this just gives you the opportunity to do a better job with your own babies! Don't fault them if they believed, and used their "right" ways, probably those were ones followed by their own parents. Times do see changes, so reassessments may be necessary.

If your parents meanly and viciously abused you, or treated you as a slave, when old enough, use your own ability to judge whether or not to follow their guidance, and to believe all they have told you. Would you honour the father who treated a child as being solely for the father's, or mother's, sexual pleasure? Such stories are now coming to light because the adults, who were abused when they were children, are telling their stories. When I was teaching at the detention centre, more than one of the girls told about leaving home because her mother had thrown her out, after she discovered that the father was using her as his lover (such abuse happen to boys too.) Where was that mother all that time? At the age of 14, what choice did that abused child have, but to earn a living as a prostitute? It was the only skill he/she had; that was the profession they had been trained for!

I remember one very sweet and innocent sixteen year old who had just been incarcerated for the first time. She cried a lot and the other older women and I tried to console her. She had had to leave when her mother found out that both her father, and his brother, expected her to be sexually available all the time, at their whims. We all tried to assure her that it was not her fault, and that she had legal recourse. Whatever happened to her . . . We were not allowed any contact once an inmate left the institution.

Another girl, whom I didn't meet until she had been on the street for quite a while, was a drug addict. She was with us many times, and would first ask to be put into "solitary" for medical supervision until the heroin left her system. She knew enough not to "go cold turkey" on the range. That was the fate of many addicts that we saw. After some very "hard time" in Kingston, I heard that this lady had had kept a baby. She decided to live away from Toronto and to settle down. I hope so. She was very bright, and had a lot of good common sense to offer to the child, and to the rest of the world.

The horror, the absolute horror of the people, who sacrifice their lives for their religion's ideas, is beyond what I can understand. Is their current situation so bad that the thought of paradise is more enticing? Are they so brainwashed that they believe their many gods need these sacrifices? For my belief system, there is a life after death, but that is for the souls who know what real LOVE is, and have practiced it in their lives. We all hope for as long a life as possible. Most of us want a long life so we can grow more in our usefulness and our understanding of LOVE. Our longevity is not up to us. I have no fear of death. I know I'm fortunate, as many people do fear death because of the old ideas of their "gods."

We may very well die slowly, enduring terrible situations. That is not for us to determine either. Sometimes it is possible for you to understand that you have made your own misery, but not very often! If you were a smoker who refused to quit, then that is inevitable. What if your death is from lung cancer and you were never even near a smoker? Death just comes sometimes! It is not up to you, nor to God. He doesn't do bad things! The end is not ours to decide. My mother had fed a family of six on a tight budget. At home, we ate very healthy food, and always enough. Treats were at a minimum. Then all of a sudden, I was my own boss as far as my food intake was concerned. I became a diabetic at the age of forty-two. It was a warning to the rest of the family who may have the same genes.

So far, I've mostly talked about the old beliefs people are questioning. They are so much a part of the present day media. What about the beliefs which are particular to men? Most males in our culture were raised to think that if they fathered a baby, then they should raise, or at least support, the child. There is a big section in the Globe and Mail recently about how very different the current situation is within the many varied cultures in Toronto.

Is this change a result of the free use of the female contraception pill? Males seem to think that since every girl is now using it, then any girl is available for their sexual use. Techniques to get this "free" sex are now being propagated. One of the obvious ways is to make sure the girl is too drunk and will not know the difference. Too many girls fall for this. I think that is rape. Another ruse is to try first to destroy the girl's image of herself so that she is grateful for any attention. Considering what the fashion industry is now doing to the female image, it is probably easy. The media is also at fault in that they portray the male image of the stud that spends his time with gorgeous ladies who continually have drinks.

I might not have taken this so seriously if I had not been exposed to the teenage party scene. One of my teaching assignments was at a high school where the homes were big, and there was extra family money for the students to enjoy. About Thursday, a rumour would be soon circulated among the "in crowd" that a party was to be held at the home of the student whose parents were in Florida that Saturday! This was a common occurrence. The only change would be the location of the party place, and where the "old folks" were spending holiday! One mother was upset when she returned home to find a pair of lacy female panties in her bed. The partiers had not cleaned up as well as they thought! It is amazing what a teacher hears when the students are bragging. (Nowadays, I expect this slander is all on the internet instead of being school gossip). Among young offenders, it was a common brag that each had many "baby mothers."

In the Muslim culture, we are now seeing another place where men seem to be questioning beliefs taught to them from the Koran. They are told in the Koran that it is wrong to kill another person; if you do so, you are responsible to look after the dependents of the victim. Some Mullahs are now justifying killing. They are telling even young men and women to be martyrs with those explosives tied to their bodies. The boys are supposedly told they will have seventy-two virgins when they reach heaven. Among all the old women I know who are in paradise; I wonder where these young boys will each find 72 virgins.

Our soldiers are teaching the new recruits in Afghanistan to shoot guns. I asked a friend, who was on that assignment, if the men he had been training were good shots. Our soldier laughed and told me that when the man pulled the trigger, he would turn his head and not look. Then he'd fire many bullets. If one should kill a person, the shooter would not be responsible, as someone else's bullet might have done the job. I wish those Muslim leaders had not questioned the original teachings of the Koran, or that the young boys had learned that they could question the "beliefs" that they were being taught.

How does one adjust to one's "new" belief system? If you've made up your mind to question old ideas, the questioning will, I hope, lead you to the belief that the most important force in the world is LOVE.

The most obvious dilemma is when you see that an old belief just needs slight changes to be acceptable for your life. My mother's rule, that I was never to do or say anything that was hurtful, doesn't always work. Sometimes, to be a loving person, you have to be tough and honest. It is obvious when you are showing children how to be less selfish. If they hurt a playmate, then there should be consequences. These consequences do not have to be anything more than embarrassment. Sometimes more is needed, and that will depend on the child. It is what all good teachers have to learn pretty fast to survive in a classroom! I think pain for pain is wrong. Adjust the consequences to what each child would value if he/she lost that toy or privilege.

Another good example of being lovingly unkind is when the situation arises and you feel that it is time to get married. We were told we were supposed to do that, remember? What if there is a marriage proposal, and there are no others on the horizon? Is it right to say, "Yes" to a marriage proposal, because you just feel sorry for yourself, or for the person doing the asking? In fact, that can, and actually has, led to disastrous situations. Practicing honesty is difficult. Out of concern for both parties, "No" is the loving answer.

I'm sure you can think of other rules imposed by societal beliefs, and rules you have long since abandoned; I try to think before I open my mouth, but don't always succeed. "Have a nice day" is not always appropriate, and it is easy to see that by the expression on the face of the recipient that he/she needed a hug, not a thoughtless remark. Sometimes societies' rules conflict for you and decisions which only you can make will arise. If you know that your friend's child is doing and selling drugs, do you tell the parents? I heard a lot of interesting jail gossip; interesting, yes, but I never repeated anything.

The end result is that nobody has the answers for you. You have to live your life as you believe is right. Remember your ideas will change too. Your circumstances will change. That mother I just mentioned as having abandoned her daughter had to choose between her child and her own survival. Was she right or wrong? What would you have done? She spoke no English and had never had a job in Canada so couldn't support herself.

Think of some women in India, whom we are now seeing have acid thrown on their faces by their own husbands. These are men who believed they have lost control. The women no longer believed in their husbands' control. Maybe they did rebel, or maybe they were just attractive and those men had heard another man say so. It would appear that these women have changed their belief system, but forgotten about their survival! I think survival comes first, but who am I to say that for you?

The questions about your belief system really arise if you are lucky enough to have time to contemplate your own death, which most of us do at my age; I have decided what is right for me. I am a serious advocate of euthanasia and of palliative care first . . . Not that the two necessarily go together. Dying in a hospital when death is prolonged must be real torture. Most hospitals can now offer such a quiet palliative care place. At Saint Michael's Hospital, my cousin had what I would call a "good" death. The family could visit as much as we liked. There were flowers around, a priest if one wished for prayers, and a musician visited and played quietly in the hall. When I sang him the hymns of our childhood, he squeezed my hand. He was at peace and passed away quietly.

I hope for you that you never face such stark choices of beliefs. We've all read stories where, faced with the decision of life or belief system, most people chose survival. I think particularly of a neighbour's father. The man had been a Christian scientist all his life. He had even insisted that his grandchildren attend such instruction. When he was faced with the question of a hospital death or help, he chose survival. Is it better to live to fight another day and to change your beliefs as he did? Only you can make your own choice. Right now, make sure that your relatives and friends know how you are thinking. Don't wait. You don't want anyone else to have that responsibility, or control.

Remember the guiding rules that Jesus left for us: love God love others love yourself. These are the basis for all other rules.

Rule 18

You Must Be Responsible for You

Most of us have realized that this is a general rule which makes common sense. As we get older we are glad that there are government pensions, and that we ourselves have put aside a nest egg to see us through in case there are unforeseen troubles. Some older people also have surpluses. We all justify this as being our reward for proper planning and hard work. Any extra is for the inheritance. Do we pat each other on the back and show off by telling about how we have had a holiday, bought a new car, cottage, and clothes ? This is evidence of greed, lust, or the desire to make others feel inadequate. This spending is not done for survival. Are we doing this to engender jealousy? It's an actual human trait, but very wrong.

This is done, in my case, with a shadow in the back of my mind. That shadow thought says I should have contributed more to those who have less. We think all my friends and I do a lot, but we could do more; I know. Why do we have this extra when so many of the people, who are slightly younger than we, are in debt? The newspapers are full of their stories. They are making far more money than we ever did, but have not planned for their old age. We hear of their surprise when told that the government may not be able to look after them in later years. In fact, today the provincial budget was the big news, and in two day's time we'll hear about the federal budget. Both promise extensive cuts. There will be job losses and no salary increases for quite some time. It means that the unions may have to accept either their own demise, or adjust their expectations.

The idea of having to take responsibility for your own care is a novel one to a lot of those who are still working. It requires a historical explanation. In the past weekend, my friend who grew up in rural, Eastern Europe, and I were talking about this situation. I grew up in rural New Brunswick. In both our situations, there was almost no extra cash or the luxuries that we now see acquired so freely.

Our parents understood that survival depended on their own efforts, and there was great pride and satisfaction in this accomplishment. In both cases, it was the mother's drive which caused the garden to be planted, and the food preserved for the winter months. In our case, eggs and fish were readily available; and we eat a lot of them! Meat of any kind was rare. For Yvonne, it was the chickens and the pig in the yard, and the community bake oven, and slaughter house. During the war, when my father was away, we spent the summers with my grandparents. There, I ate really well from my grandfather's huge garden; it was his pride. After his family grew up, he still kept it and sold the extra. There was never any waste of cash because it was understood that doctors cost money, and the grandparents might need medical help in their old age. They didn't live long enough to see the advent of the Canadian Medicare System.

In other words, being careful and saving money used to be for survival, as well as for security. There was a justifiable pride in being able to say that your house was paid for, that your children never went hungry, and there was extra money in the bank. It represented a sacrifice, and a lot of hard work. You would not expect that your parents would just give you a house when you got married; this had happened to two couples on our street.

I believe there is a lot to be said for taking responsibility for yourself, and meeting your life's obligations. We made it clear to our little girl that she was to do her very best in school to be equipped to earn a living. We knew we might not be around to help her, and she had no siblings. She understood this.

What really bothers me is bragging when it is about inherited wealth, especially when I can see that it is done to impress, and thus create jealousy. I'm referring to hearing a person telling about the things they inherited, or perhaps saying that their investments did so well in the market that a bigger house for entertaining is essential. Are they going to have a lot of charity events to raise money for their pet project? or . . . Are they intending to make all the people who come to visit feel awe and jealousy? If these visitors were made to feel envious and insecure, what good was accomplished? Do the owners of the big house need to cause pain to feel secure and important themselves?

It is great to believe that you have been independent and looked after yourself, and completed the obligations you accepted. You know you are secure in yourself. I learned this from my husband. If you can't say this, make major changes in your approach to life. There are many of these helpful services advertised at banks and companies which sell investment plans; just be careful. There are cheats operating as helpers as well. It is probably best to take good stock of the people who are your close friends and relatives. Ask them, but not the ones you know who are in debt, and the ones who brag may not even be the best to consult. Judge for yourself those who seem to be getting along without too many problems. They don't brag; they just seem to be quietly enjoying what life has to offer, and do not have disasters of their own making. Everyone has had and will have occasional difficulties. Be prepared.

The feeling of security and contentment is even greater when you know that what you did with any extra money made a difference to others in the world. It is even a greater feeling when you don't need to tell everyone. You just keep it inside. Believe me. When you see a person with a happy face, you just know he/she has such a happy secret. I learned that from my father. It was his habit. I'll tell of one incident where, on his meagre pensions, he gave enough money to establish a home for abused women in St. Catherine's. We learned about this after he had died.

Use your money wisely. I'll close with a poem written by my father: A good deed done, and then forgotten Will grow in the heart to such a blossom Of smiles and sweetness . . . That all who see Will know the good person But not the good deed!

Rule 19

You Must Always Be the Ant; Never Be the Grasshopper

Once upon a time in a land far away, when the animals could talk to each other. Even the insects understood each other. It was a bright and sunny summer day and the bugs were all out to appreciate the weather. None was having as much fun as the grasshopper as he bounced around on his powerful hind legs, rubbed them together, and serenaded the ladies with his beautiful voice.

After he had decided that he was the most gorgeous creature around, he looked down deep into the grass and spotted a black ant. "Oh my, aren't you the ugliest thing I've ever seen! Why are you carrying the huge piece of green leaf?"

The ant resisted the impulse to just tell him that he was about the rudest thing she'd ever seen. She had been raised according to the understood rule that duty came before fun. She hoped that she might improve the world by explaining to him that she was a worker, and that she believed that it was her "job" to help her fellow ants. She told him that the green leaves would provide food for the other ants in her nest, and for the future generations. Then she said, "I am sorry, but I don't have time to talk longer; I must do this before the snow comes so we ants have food to survive over the winter."

The grasshopper was appalled. He told her she was crazy and that she only had one life and she should really enjoy it. Convinced he was correct, he bounced off and had fun. His lady friends were glad he was back! They all agreed he was a great guy for a party! The winter came. He froze to death.

We were certainly told this fable when we were children. Usually, it was at the appropriate time when we complained about the "jobs" we were expected to do. I was the eldest of four children in my family, so there was always something I could help with. It didn't take too many brains to learn that one never said to my mother, "I'm bored." Her reply was, "If you can't find something to do, I can."

None of this had a damaging effect on me; I'm sure! Even although my daughter was an only child, she got much the same treatment. My excuse was that I held a full time job and needed her to do her bit. I'd explain that her life might not always be easy, and that she really did need to know how to wash dishes and keep the house clean. She liked cooking a lot more than the cleaning. I liked the fact that she accepted that life means shouldering one's responsibilities. She is now passing on this work ethic!

So, now, how about the good old saying, "All work, and no play, makes Jack a dull boy"? Must we always do jobs exclusively and not have fun? What if you end up in bed at night, and have had no pleasure during the day? You could say to yourself that you have the satisfaction of knowing what you did was right. Do you then feel resentment? If you can honestly say that the day was okay, then who am I to judge? If you can't say you feel alright about the one life God gave you, you are making a mistake. A satisfying life does need balance between work and play.

I'll grant you that there is a lot of satisfaction in knowing that you have lived by your ideals of what is right and wrong, and you've done your appointed or assumed jobs. I really pity the people who are unemployed and want so much to work. Believe me they aren't having fun with all that spare time. The smarter people, though, are finding it is best to use the free time to try to improve their job skills, and to work at a small paying project, if that is possible.

When you have survived an economic depression as did my parents and grandparents, this is not an issue. If you wanted to eat and live, you worked. People did die. There was no social assistance. There were, of course, very few paying jobs in this period in history, but if you could see that a farmer needed help with his crops, you helped. You knew he could not pay cash, but perhaps he'd give you a few eggs from his chickens or a few potatoes from his field. People just did that. There was a pride in saying that the family never starved all through the depression. My grandfather and my father-in-law were able to use their skills to work. They walked miles for only a dollar or two a day and were paid only when the owner got his money. We've recently seen on TV, and in the papers, that some unemployed workers are complaining about how they might have to go away to get a job. Granted, in some ways the depression was easier because more of us were living on the land and had gardens. I worry about people in the cities today. What would those living in apartments do for necessities?

Those in my generation could probably be self-sustaining. Maybe my daughter's generation wouldn't be so badly off as they have seen gardens, and do know what work is. Would my grandchildren be okay? I just hope so. The bottom line here is that, for survival, duty must come before pleasure. The Ant is right. There is a big *but*, however. We still have grasshoppers, don't we? Does God really look after all the happy irresponsible fools? I certainly know of people who are in this category, and they do seem to get by. (Perhaps they just hide their suffering). Why then am I saying that we should put duty first?

The best answer I can give is that you have to live with yourself, and could you do that if you didn't do what you believed was "right"? I go back to the dilemma presented in the Charles Dickens book, <u>Oliver</u>. Most children do personify this innate understanding of "right and not right." They instinctively know when they are mistreated and that what is done to them is not right. It takes a lot of teaching to convince a little one to do what is "not right"! Oliver had to be taught to steal. Remember that horrible advertisement on TV where the little boy is handed a cardboard truck instead of the one he thought he was promised. His reply, "It's a piece of junk!" was right on the mark. He knew what was right.

Is there anything that can justify "guilty" pleasures? Not if "it" makes you feel guilty! How can you have any fun in life if that is the case? How much guilt can you live with? Are you hurting anyone? Are you hurting yourself? Are you hurting yourself because you believe you deserve it? That's self-flagellation. You decide. God, who is LOVE, has said we must love ourselves. I believe He wants you to have fun.

Duty first was usually regarded as the way to success and happiness throughout life. Didn't thousands of soldiers die in two world wars just because they strongly believed it was their duty to defend Canada, and Great Britain's honor? My father felt the duty strongly and signed up the day our government said it would support England. I grew up without a father for most of World War II. I did not, as a result, live under the dictatorship of Hitler. What was my father's duty? Did he do what was right? When he saw war protesters marching on TV, he had tears in his eyes. He'd say, "Don't tell me that my friends died for nothing." Was, and is war right? I'm sure God wants peace for us. If we could avoid such conflicts, we would not have such awful news every night on TV. We would not have such a controversy about spending our resources on weapons, and those expensive bombers. We could then replace the old army trucks so they could be available to help in times of natural disasters!

Hence, I have arrived at the dilemma of "good" versus "evil." Far better minds than mine have discussed this, yet have not solved the problem of how we should live with "evil." Jesus acknowledged the evil in our world. It was the jealousy of His power that led to His death. The leaders, both Roman and Jewish, had felt their control to be threatened by Him. They had to get rid of Jesus. If only we could convince our world leaders to aim for the good of their citizens, instead of engaging in their expensive acquisition of power. Men with their envy and covetousness produce evil happenings.

I would not want to be a politician. Power is an attractive, but a corrupting force. We do have a few men who are honestly in government for the good they can do. I think of poor Ken Dryden. He and his family have done so much good with their project of *Sleeping children around the world*. Money from Canadians, with the help of Rotary International, makes it possible for bed kits, to be distributed to the children of the isolated villages in places like India, Latin America and Africa. He was defeated in the last election, and is now threatened with a personal debt. I believe he was one who just felt it was his duty to help his country. I believe God truly wants us to do our duty, and love and help one another. How can we convince all leaders not to wish for power, but for peace? If you wish to be a leader, then your duty is to take up this challenge. There is nothing in your accepting the task that says one can't have fun while doing this. I think that Hillary Clinton is doing more than her duty, but I also believe that it is what she sees as her personal fulfillment. For quite a lot of people that is the right life, maybe it is her "fun."

On a smaller scale is a friend who has a very responsible job on a contract with the federal government. She organizes sites abroad for the interviewing of prospective educated clients for jobs in Canada. Her staff checks their qualifications, language skills, and tell them about possible Canadian placements that are available here. She likes visiting places she hasn't been before. Also, she is a runner and likes to do that in different places, except in Mumbai—even in the mornings there is too much smog!

Yes, do your duty . . . but enjoy life and have fun too!

Rule 20

You Must Act if You Have
Accepted a Responsibility

The discussions in the last two "rules" bring up the question of accepting what one considers one's responsibilities in life. I've been talking about the concept of a "duty" which I define as moral responsibility. There are, however, those challenges which we agree to accept that are not necessarily moral duties, but choices that we make. Considering the larger scene, some of us think we have enough to do to keep ourselves alive. We admire those who agree to take on the larger tasks, and wish them well. We say that they must be smarter and more capable than we are, and that we allow them to be. Thinking "small" is always "safer." Can you even imagine what would have happened if Churchill had thought this "small way" and had not taken on and not acted on his perceived responsibilities during the war? People who agree to see the bigger picture, and accept such responsibility have my greatest admiration.

In this case I'll tell you of a teacher friend who has taken on the job of being a vice-principal at a difficult school. At this time, she also has major home responsibilities. I know her well enough to know that she is coping with it all very well. She is more than capable. She loves herself too. This summer she and her family will be enjoying a trip to Asia.

We all have the responsibilities that accrue in our lives if we have even the smallest contact with our fellow human beings. Unless we have decided to live as hermits or for ourselves alone, we face the choice of how much the obligations control our lives, and how much of our time and energy can be devoted to what we feel we "deserve in life." For many there is no question here. If our survival depends on us completing our obligations, then we do what is required. We see the mothers in Africa walking miles for help for their starving children. It is only in North America, and not even in all areas here, where we feel we can have lives apart from our jobs, or our families. Do we even realize our good luck?

We all know of people who took on a responsibility, and then shirked it. They gave their word and then did not follow through. Others were depending on them. In the case of a soldier in a battle in the First World War, if he ran away, his own superiors shot him as a deserter. In our time, nothing that drastic happens.

There are fathers who agreed to have children and then "disappeared." They are major shirkers. Of course, yet they are truly the losers as they never see and enjoy the rewards and challenges of fatherhood. I've known of mothers who did the same. I don't understand. Did they believe they had no responsibility for the baby? Within my lifetime, young mothers were actually forced by their own parents, or government social workers to surrender their babies for adoption. Some of our friends were very grateful for those sacrifices. Nowadays, such mothers have a choice. In some cases, they are allowed to share the parenting with adoptive parents. These people must be a very special loving couple.

Most adults in Canada now have the choice of whether or not to have children. If we do reproduce, and if we feel it is becoming too much of a burden, most of us still struggle on. This can be a real challenge, especially for the teenage parents. We now miss the ceremonies that other societies have to stress to the teenagers that when they become adults, they should take care of themselves and accept their responsibilities! We don't do that today because we want our teens to have enough education, or training so that it is possible for them to earn a living. One young boy returned from a big Bar Mitzvah party wishing he could be Jewish! We should create such a rite of passage. Some teens do feel the need.

Whether or not the parents stay together, most people believe that it is their responsibility to support their child, both financially and emotionally. Is it a duty? If there is a divorce, then the responsibility should fall on both mother and father. All of this is usually settled by agreements and by lawyers. I think the shared parenting model sounds good, but I'm not involved, so who am I to judge? Remember the wisdom of Solomon, who used the threat of the sword to decide the "real" parent's identity? So, whether in a settled home, or a separated one, children should also learn to accept responsibilities. It is good training, and it helps them to appreciate what their parents do for them. Completion of tasks is essential. Ensuring even that is a job for a parent!

Once, our daughter was invited to go on a vacation with another family. We knew the family and agreed, but made it clear that we expected her to earn money to pay her way. We gave her two hundred as a Christmas gift. She wasn't quite sixteen. She did earn the money. It was not a cheap trip. To do this she took on the summer job of minding the local little boy who was so naughty that we all called him, "No, Joe!" That was the only name we'd ever heard his mother say.

I also want you to know the story of a very dear friend. She was part of a large Polish family who were sent to England as refugees during, or after, World War II. The family consisted of six girls and the parents. The oldest girl was fortunate to be able to take training as a hairdresser in England. She decided to come to Canada as soon as she could, and once she was here she worked hard at her profession. As soon as she accumulated money, she brought the rest of the family to her new home. All are successful here. They are good citizens, glad to be here, and thankful to their "big sister." She never married, but is happily settled in her own lovely home. I admire her so much for her accepting what she saw as her responsibility, and acting on it. Was it her moral duty? No, she had a choice and chose to take on that responsibility. It was the one decision she could live with and be contented.

There can be real problems of assigning responsibilities to children if the parents were raised in different cultures. There can even be problems when you both had basically the same background. In some cultures, the roles of the mother and father are very clearly defined. I tried to explain to my friends from Iraq that here in Canada men also change diapers. The boys didn't think so!

When problems arise within a marriage, both parties previously had agreed to certain commitments and responsibilities. They should each remember that. People don't stop maturing and changing as time passes. If there are no discussions and no give and take, then there will be no resolutions. It must be extremely sad and hurtful when one partner just leaves without an obvious reason. The one who is left deserves to be able to understand so he/she can live in peace. That, at least, was the responsibility of the person who left, or was he/she a person who never understood that the good things in life usually come with responsibilities.

Sometimes in areas other than marriage, you might accept a responsibility that is beyond your ability or strength. To admit this is not a failure. It is only a failure if you continue, and do not move aside and make space for the next person in line who can "fill those shoes." We all meet such life situations. In the press we hear of many cases where the person in political life should have stepped down, but felt he/she had to save his/her precious ego. One sees these failures in businesses as well. Maybe even in our parliament! Do you really want a story about you in the news? Letting go is often the noble and honourable thing to do. Don't be ashamed. Use your gifts in which you excel. At the end of your life, you'll be happy as well as admired.

Remember, you only have one life and it is yours to control. Accept and complete the responsibilities to which you have agreed. Complete your moral duties as you understand them. It is my hope that this will make for your peaceful death. I must wait to see if this idea works!

Rule 21

You Must Listen to Your Fears

What is "fear"? What is meant by being "safe"? Using the Canadian Oxford Dictionary, the word "fear" means an unpleasant emotion caused by threat of danger or pain. The word, 'safe" means secure, protected from danger or pain. According to these definitions, they are indeed opposites. Consequently, if you want to avoid any danger, or pain, or suffering, or unpleasantness, you use common sense and heed your fear. There are people who follow this rule to the letter. They never do anything. They are very safe indeed! But, are they really that safe? Do they suffer? Yes! Can one really live like this? Some do. The agony of always worrying is very hard on one physically. I used to refuse to deal realistically with all fears!

Since I've made it clear that I am discussing a freer culture than the one which demands a total burqa, I'll restrict my discussion of fear as it refers to all restrictive cultures, including mine which had the rules I'm discussing and which I was raised with. I can't talk about the topic without a note of sympathy for these women who are forced to wear that complete covering, and for the many that can't leave the privacy of their homes without a male companion. My perception is they must live in total fear and subjugation. Where is the love? Are they safe? Are they being protected? Are they being abused? Maybe it depends on the nature of the man who has that extreme control over them. Is this control from the home? From the Taliban in Afghanistan? From religious leaders? From their own belief systems?

I know that I can't live with constant fear, so I'll choose to examine where, in Canada, fear comes from for me, and how I deal with it head on. My answers may not be any use to you, but in case it is a bit of help, I'll explain anyway. I grade my fears into categories: physical, mental, emotional, and spiritual. At the moment, the physical fear is very much to the fore. I've had knee problems for over six years. This causes me to fall and to do physical damage, such as break bones and have spectacular bruises. The solution was to have the knee replacement. With our "free" health care, one waits a long time for elective surgery. The surgeon did a new knee for me on October 1, ten months later. I did not anticipate the mini-stroke a day later, but all is coming along well and I'm so glad I agreed to have the operation. Sure I was scared, but I faced the pain because I knew my life was already better afterward. It is!

I've talked to strong grown men whose physical fear means they can't face a needle, even if it means it could help them avoid serious medical problems. It is beyond my understanding that I get this reaction when I suggest they should get the newly available needle for the disease, shingles. It is available now for older people. It will stop the complications, such as losing sight, which can happen if the shingles virus gets into the eyes. Some people are really refusing this chance to avoid shingles' suffering. I've seen too much of it to comprehend their refusal because of fear of one small needle. Where does this fear come from? Did the mother make a big fuss about medical procedures when the child was young? What a disservice that would be! This is one case where I see nothing wrong with a bribe. Bribes work.

I've also heard of people dying because they feared the pain of the cure. There are those who'd prefer the pain of arthritis to the pain of a "fix." Sometimes there is a solution; maybe they are afraid to take pills, which will keep the inflammation in check. I think of a friend who is dead now. He would refuse to take the pills for diabetes if anyone was around. We had dinner last night with a couple we've been friends with for a short while. The lady mentioned that she had trouble with a cataract in her left eye. She was scared to have any doctor cut that tissue, and so she will put off the operation. I assured her that I had both eyes done and will never again be blinded. My vision is perfect. What a blessing! Meeting physical fear head on pays off.

Next, is how does one cope with a physical fear that is combined with mental fear? It takes real courage, and time to adapt to the idea that there is the proverbial "light" at the end. My strength I've mentioned is nothing. I see the real strength and courage when I hear the stories and pictures of the men and women who are coping with their recoveries from their terrible war injuries. They have suffered both physical and mental anguish in Iraq and Afghanistan. In previous wars, they would have died of their wounds. Are we doing them a favor by offering them life? We are if they have the faith in themselves. I think even more courage is demanded of those wounded who also have posttraumatic stress disorder (PTSD). It must make coping with the physical healing much harder. Here the courage required is great. Constant loving help is terribly important. The initial challenge might even be that one would have to convince the doctor that he/she even had a PTSD problem. Recently, there was a former army pilot who went berserk and refused to continue flying his plane at 30,000 feet. Had he tried to talk a doctor? Had he been told to just pull himself together? We may never know. The co-pilot and other passengers saved the day. Did he then get the help he needed?

We will never know how many of these cases are just self-diagnosed, and then alcohol is applied as the solution. They are so much happier when "loaded" they convince themselves that that is the cure. The soldiers who suffered from PTSD after World War II are a case in point. They used alcohol to fight the nightmares. I know it because we had two veterans in the family who did that. Not only did they continue to have horrendous mental fears, but for people living with those men, life was sometimes very difficult. Thankfully, now it is a recognized problem, and in the United States, there are clinics. For some, however, the help was too late. One night we saw a programme about the homeless men on the streets in the USA. A lot of them were dysfunctional because of the stress of the Vietnam War. Now there is progress for those cases too. People are trying to identify them, and place them in homes where help is available. How many of the 'street people" in Canada are in similar positions, yet get no help?

There are other mental problems which are now being identified. A friend's daughter has been identified as being dyslectic and having dyspraxia. When I saw the list of traits for these handicaps, I was amazed. I have struggled with these problems all my life. There are real mental fears here; I know! I always referred to myself as being a stupid speller. The letters were never in the right order and the "b" and the "d" just wouldn't go in their proper places and make themselves the right way around! I'd wonder why so many of my arithmetic answers were wrong. Arithmetic is hard when one copies the numbers in reverse! I had a lot of tears about that after the other students had all gone home.

I thought I was spastic when it came to sports. That is what dyspraxia means. For any physical activity, the right and left brains have to be programmed to get connected by many repetitions of the physical pattern. It was hard for me to learn to make a turn on skis; I finally got it. Then all the women in the class cheered, "Yeah, Barb!" a good experience for a teacher! Now, I could understand my students better.

Another mental problem which cause a lot of fear and which experts are now identifying, and hoping to learn to cope with, is the fetal alcohol syndrome. This is the damage caused by the mother's abuse of alcohol while she is pregnant. Often she'll drink because of her emotional fear of not coping socially. It bothers me, for this reason, when I see so many young teens thinking that being drunk is the only way to have fun. They must still believe, as we did at that age, that it made them more loveable! Are the girls, especially girls, still so silly? For a long time no one realized the terrible intellectual problems for the fetus, that a mother's drinking during pregnancy caused. Now, it can be almost a joke for the "thinking woman." If she is out with her friends, and she refuses even the glass of wine, they all tease and say, "We know why!" They did, however, go on to congratulate her. No thinking pregnant woman drinks!

Teaching the child with fetal alcohol syndrome requires a lot of patience. I know because I've taught reading to more than one such child. Hopefully, they were born before women knew of the potential danger. Many of these children fail to cope with the challenges of life. They frequently do not connect cause and effect. Consequently, the pain, which follows a punch, is regarded with surprise and shock. This leads to being in trouble, and often to jail. Feeling at home in jail could be a result. At present, we have no idea how many of the men and women in our jails are burdened by this problem. These 'socially handicapped" people have a real social fear that people will find out about their deficiency. Even applying for a job is frightening. I certainly met them. I think of one in particular who, somehow, had learned to read, but for whom math concepts were impossible. She said that she trusted her customers when she sold them drugs as she could not tell the difference between one-fourth and one-half.

The jails have many other inmates who have been identified with other problems, problems which have been called, in that setting, "emotional." These are really related to the fears which were probably not identified when they were children, and which were never treated. If a child is abused as an infant and/or as a toddler, the physical and mental fears can be very debilitating. How can one learn self-control, when one sees the adults in the house are showing no restraint? As with the PTSD soldiers, these wounded people may have had to resort to socially unacceptable means to stay alive.

Whatever their solution was, the institutional care for all these people is minimal at best. Is doing nothing really the safest solution for them and for the public? The authorities seem to lack courage to face the problems. What are the administrators" fears? Do they think, as many politicians seem to, that we all should regard those who break the laws as undeserving of any help? We do need to improve inmate care, but maybe it is as my husband says when I raise the issue, "The general public is just relieved when they are locked up, and when the little old ladies and children are safe." The jail solution is a waste of taxpayer's money, and of human life!

We should have the courage to treat the serious addiction cases and emotional cases where we find them. If we don't, then they produce more children with such problems. Inmates with emotional difficulties were getting a little help at The Toronto West Detention Centre; there was a psychiatrist who visited those who requested his attention. There were church services, and guards who were cognoscente enough, and kind enough, to identify such people and place them in special ranges (living areas). It was assumed that they would get better care if they went to serve sentences in the regular jails. Did they? I doubt it.

Kind listeners on a one-to-one basis are required. One of my friends did this for at least 20 years; she was a volunteer. One day, she inadvertently gave an inmate questionable material as an aid to his learning to read. She was told never to return. I personally know of men and women with whom she had a bond. Although we were never allowed to have any contact after they left the centre, we'd later hear via the jail gossip that they were off the streets and doing well. Who knows? I know that she made a very real difference for one man who was deported at his request after he was found innocent. Thanks to her, he returned to his country speaking and reading English.

I know a lot of the students that I had, both in jail and in regular schools who just needed a chance to talk. They needed to have someone to listen without criticising. Trained therapists get a lot of money for that service! If your fear-based problem is not as severe as an emotional breakdown, like the one that pilot had, a listening and kind friend is needed. Don't do "nothing." Find a listening friend. You usually know the solution and just need to hear yourself say it out loud. Do something. What? You don't have such a friend? Why?

What causes this social fear of close friendships? I understand it is very real to them. Are they afraid of damage to their egos? Are they so insecure that if someone discovered a fault in their personalities, they believe that person would make fun, or tell others? Can these fearful people not accept that they probably have weaknesses, as we all do? Can they not laugh at themselves? If this is you, read more of my writing. A good person, who will listen, can literally be a lifesaver. I have several friends on whom I "lean." I will speak later about how to accumulate these friends. You do need more than one confidant as they tend to move, or at my age, I find they tend to die.

The spiritual and final fear, the biggest of all, is the fear of death. I told you about my close friend, Mary. Go back and read it again because she certainly went through what many who face imminent death will go through. I truly do not have this problem. Why? I faced it myself long ago when I realized that I had diabetes. It is a death sentence. I had always questioned a lot of the doctrines of any church, but now I have found a belief system which works for me.

I've found, moreover, that in my present place of worship there are many situations where I feel very at home and very comforted. What I also did was to accumulate quite a large library of books about the beginnings of the Christian church. I learned a lot.

Rule 22

You Must Maintain All Ingrained Prejudices

When my child was little, my husband and I made an honest effort to keep any prejudices we were raised with to ourselves. We were conscious of being polite and friendly to all people we met, and of encouraging her to be the same. One day when she was about four and we were driving, we saw a hitchhiker. I did not stop. There was a silence and then the little voice said, "We don't pick up hitchhikers, do we?" There was a pause, then there was the remark, "We don't like people who are dirty. Do we?" I've forgotten how I handled that, but it did bring me up short to realize that I did have such a prejudice, and that I had instilled it in her mind.

What good do our prejudices do us? They make us feel superior to the person we believe is inferior. It is the old saying, "Thank God I'm not as "bad" as he/she is!" The next thought is that the person could change, and be as "good" as me, if he/she really wanted to. Therefore, we feel it is okay to consider them not our equal because they don't make the effort to "improve" to our standard. Hence, we falsely build our own egos, and in so doing we make ourselves into people who are not very likeable; make ourselves into people who really do not have as many "real" friends as we probably would wish for.

There's been a lot in the media recently about the horrors of bullying. I am so grateful that it is finally coming to the attention of the people who have some power to affect a change. I saw so much of it as a teacher. If a parent was approached about his/her child's being a bully, it was denied. Now perhaps the teacher working with the parent can really help, that is so important for that abusive child, maybe even more so than for the child who was picked on. That child who was the victim did often feel isolated, and wanted that negative attention. He/she was usually different in some way, and the prejudices of the bully were being exercised. The ultimate result, we now understand, could lead to the suicide of the victim. If it is not death, I still believe that a life time of internalizing the feeling of inferiority can just be as damaging. It requires much love and encouragement to restore a sense of worth and build a positive identity. For one young man I know well, it took lots of love and counselling over several years. He is now a very successful, confident businessman.

Back to my problem with "dirty" people; it was real. We who live in North America will have no trouble in understanding that being clean makes you more socially acceptable, and prevents diseases as well. We have lots of water, and it has been emphasized to us for generations that if you are clean, then you will not get ill as often, as do people in countries with limited water. *Cleanliness is next to Godliness!* We seem gradually to be acknowledging that our water is probably our most important resource. Yet, we still do not take this seriously, and as my husband has often said, "Why should we worry? We live beside Lake Ontario."

We do realize that it is not an easy job for people who live on the street to stay healthy. One of their biggest problems is not being able to wash. This is one cause of the prejudice, which we are now facing, against street persons. There is no easy solution, and it is not a popular discussion for city councils. In Vancouver, we have recently heard about their idea of special, small, individual apartments for such people. The buildings are run by the government, and the rent is reasonable. The social workers and the health workers visit often, and hope to be able to give back to the person some of his/her self-respect. Every once in a while, we hear of another city hoping to try this, but the cost apparently makes it almost impossible to establish the large number of rooms, which would be required. Because of that false economy, these people continue to cost us much more money, as they inevitably end up in expensive care in hospitals.

Fortunately, nowadays, there has even been some progress in the acceptance of gay relationships in Canada. It has become common knowledge that such persons are born with this genetic difference, which can be seen in their brain scans. Being openly gay is, therefore, 'socially acceptable." However, many people still require a lot of persuasion, particularly in my generation. I remember all the talking I had to do with a mother I knew very well. She persisted in her personal prejudice, no matter what. She'd say, "But she could try to change!" No, she could not! It is no longer an issue. She is now married and in a happy, loving relationship. Both women are leading very productive lives, and looking forward to happy retirements. It makes me content and happy for her, as I love her so much. The same applies to male couples who are my friends, two of whom I know well. Their relationships are no different from those of heterosexual couples. There is the division of labor, as we have, and the same disagreements. There is also much respect and love. If one person is in trouble, such as experiencing an illness, his partner is right there to support.

The troubles with racial and religious prejudices keep surfacing in North America. I am glad that they are no longer ignored, but dealt with full force by our laws, our courts, and our free press. Reporters are now travelling, and reporting the problems around the world, and the world is paying attention. Is this awareness the cause of the Arab Spring, and of those upheavals? I believe it is. Tribal societies often foster such prejudicial ideas to keep the members of the group together.

Is the transfer to other countries of our ideas of "human rights" and democracy the right thing for us to be doing? It seems to be leading to a lot of bloodshed. Could we stop this tide if we choose? No. Is it right? I guess only time will tell. I do think that all people want the right to lead their own lives. First, however, they have to have security of life for them and for the children. There is an account of the results of the voting in Libya, the first in years. It appears that there are many parties, which have won seats, and not just the religious ones. Now, it will be a real test to see if those divisions can be solved, as obviously there are many prejudices involved!

Do I have any other prejudices? I was asked that once by a student. I had to ponder before I answered. I believe that I've let go of the usual ones. I did, though, have to confess to thinking that I feel very angry when I see a person with one certain character trait. I get upset with people, who have a lot of life chances, potential, and ability, then waste their gifts by being lazy, by doing nothing, or by getting high or drunk. To me, they are despicable. They upset me. I don't care how many, or how few natural gifts you have; just use them. Contribute something; preferably do some good, help someone!

I'm not sure I should conquer this prejudice. It would be nice if I could help these people find fulfillment. I know I should.

Sometimes I can't, as I believe that it is their prerogative to waste their gifts. They, however, in so doing, make loving them, as I should, very difficult. That is my problem! I could not live the way they do. I want friends who love me and accept me as I am; warts and all, even with this prejudice.

Rule 23

You Must Accept the Criticism of Others

Most of us really do willingly accept others "put-downs" without a second thought. We tend to think we have to do so. Maybe we wish to please the speaker, and gain his/her friendship and/or respect. "If I were you, I wouldn't wear that color. It makes you look sick, older, and not sexy and so on." "That was a stupid thing to say!" "Why did you choose: that house, that furniture, that wife?" The list is endless, and some people believe they actually have the right to say such things! The worst are the comments about the perceived troubles you may be having with your offspring. Can you resist heeding their "advice" and not be hurt by their implied criticism of your parenting, and also not worry about losing their "valuable" friendship?

It gets easier to reject the negative comments as one gets older, but I still hear them and think about them. If you are young and insecure, it is almost impossible to hear and not respond to the remarks directed at you. We are now realizing, as a society, the stress such criticism places upon many teenagers. Teens don't usually have the self-assurance to realize that the person who is so critical is just wishing to boost his/her own self-confidence by showing up the weakness in someone else. It is the reason that parents should never give up their parenting until he/she is well assured that a child has reached real maturity. By this, I mean, that he/she has enough self-belief to weather these 'storms."

I realize that many parents heave a sigh of relief when the child hits the teens, and that they want to have chances for their own pursuits. It is a great temptation to say, "Now is my time. My child can look after him/herself." No no no! This is the time for regular talks and listening. Question only if they seem to be on the wrong track, but you'll never know if you don't listen. I turned off talking to my parents when I thought that my mother was far too interested in lecturing, and in her own social pursuits than she was in my life. My father, of course, was far too busy with his work! Teens are still very narcissistic and need to be shown, even more than before, that they come first in your life . . . even when they are being obnoxious! Most of them are struggling to be independent and "grown up." This is probably the hardest time to act the role of the understanding, mature parent. Mothers who have not been able to practice their professions can be tempted to think it is okay to give up the reins. No!

Do you know who was with your "child" last Saturday night? Was there a party with a lot of drinking, or sex, and/or drugs? Were the parents home? How many other teens are heeding the criticism of their peers and suffering without even one adult being aware? I think, because of the number teens with whom I have talked, that there are many who need the ear of a mature adult. I used to sit in my classroom after school, supposedly to get my marking done. The students knew I'd be there. One time a boy of eighteen came in a rush, slammed the door and burst into tears. "I'm going to kill myself!" was his greeting. I took a chance and didn't even open that door. I just stood and hugged him until he calmed down, and could actually talk. I could have been fired. I had no choice! And he is still alive!

A short while ago, I was involved in all the funeral gatherings for the death of a young person killed in a car accident. I heard in the voices and saw on Facebook the agony of her friends. She had been the one they went to with their troubles. Yes, teens do try to comfort each other, and so few have the inner resources to be such a help. She had had that gift. Their sense of grief and loss were palpable. Even if I was a stranger to most of them, they would cry in my arms as I hugged them. She had even written to the ones who were in jail, and often she would be the only one with whom they corresponded!

I know that some of my "friends' need and want listeners, as did this student. There is always a need for people who have willing ears and the time. Sometimes, just the opening question, "How are you?' is sufficient to bring on a flood of tears. Sometimes it is a kind voice and a hug, which will enable you to break through. To do this you need to put your own worries "on hold." You must, however, recognize that you too need listeners. When you find that loving friend, those rewarding exchanges will be mutual. That is a "real friendship." Such is my friend, Edyth.

Yes, even with my dyslexia, I finally learned that that is the spelling she has for her name on her birth certificate, and I am supposed to use it. We have known each other for over forty years and been through a lot of problems with husbands, children, and friends. I have always known that I could go to her for wise advice, and for an abundance of LOVE. I believe that she feels the same about my unconditional love. If she ever reads this, she'll laugh, but will also truly understand. We can be blunt with each other if there is a controversy; then we agree to disagree. She has many such friends. These people usually do. I believe it is because all her friends sense that she loves herself enough to give her attention and time to us. She had wonderful parents who gave love to her. What a gift! So, do you want to be this type of person whom the world loves? How do you accomplish that? Read "Rule 24."

Friendship is not something you can buy, bribe, threaten, or embarrass a person. These methods may get you subservience and grudging respect, but never a real loving friend. Do you want fame, or money? Or do you want this LOVE?

Remember the words, "Where your heart is; there will your treasure be also." Look for LOVE in friends who offer it. The critical people should be limited to the penalty box. Give them a little time and then ask them why they said what they said to you. It is also okay to suggest that they themselves may need a special ear. Offer yours if they wonder about their own problems. It'll either cause them to flee, or to break down in tears. They may never have had such an offer!

You Must Not Let People Get Too Close

That rule is wrong, wrong, wrong! You truly can never have too many friends. Don't be afraid of others. There really is no law against being a sharing, loving friend. Now, I am finding it is best to have them in abundance, in many age brackets! I attend too many funerals. I also realize it is more interesting to be with friends of different backgrounds, educational levels, various employments, as well as various ages. I want it clear at the start of this discussion, however, that there is nothing like an old friend who loves you and accept you for yourself, a person with whom you have a history. You've shared fun and sorrows and a philosophy of life; he/she was there when you were in need, and vice versa.

If you don't have as many friends as you desire, abandon those old rules I've been discussing. Are you insufferable? If your behaviour, speech, actions are perfect, then maybe you are that person without "faults," and that is almost inexcusable. Stop! Let down your guard. Ask yourself, are you causing the ones around you to feel resentful and inferior? Reach out; they also need friends, not critics. So, how do you let down that guard, that wall of perfect behaviour?

Are you insecure to the point of being over sensitive to hints or suggestions that other people make? Does their criticism hurt your feelings? If so, be aware that while such people may think they are helpful, that may not be their real intention. Take a good look. Do they really care, or are they trying to make you feel inadequate so that, by comparison, they boost their own self-images? It might be a situation such as this, "I think you should not wear that style as it makes you look older." Are they really a good judge of your personal style?

Are they acting this way because they have they been told by someone that their own choice of clothing was not good? Are they feeling insecure and wishing that you'd feel the same? Always take the circumstances into consideration. My husband dislikes the words, "you should." Nothing guarantees better than do those words that he'll not take the advice. Watch that you are not guilty yourself of doing this to people. Try always to make people feel good about themselves. "You truly catch more flies with honey, than with vinegar." Anyone who talks to you in this fashion often needs friends more than you do. Is this really, a kind of person, you want in your life?

Keep the problems of others you hear about to yourself. Make an honest effort never to tell what's been heard, even if it is the most exciting piece of gossip. Once I knew about the problem my friend Sue had had, and she had solved it successfully. I introduced her to a person with a similar difficulty. That second lady stopped talking, and I got a scolding afterwards. She really did need help, but because she couldn't share, she never got the help. They both lost the possibility of having a new real friend because that second person wasn't open to offer help.

Be a good listener, and the closest friends are the ones who will give you a turn to talk and will listen to you. Children learn this quality feature of friendship from their parents when they are little. As a parent, most of us realize a child's need for us to listen forever: to their dreams and nightmares, their fears and successes. As I said earlier, it doesn't matter how old you are, a friend's undivided attention is very precious.

How many people are there in the world, who need this listening care? I think now of the young person, who died, and who had given her time to her friends. The age doesn't matter. I have a lot of young friends, but I've gained a few more since I retired. These youthful contacts have kept my thinking young. We all need different influences if we are not to let our ideas age with us. The youth organizations all are in desperate need of mature help. Consider such volunteering. You'll be surprised what you learn and how much you gain . . . maybe even a new friend.

There may even be people whom you now refer to as your acquaintances, people who need listeners. Perhaps you've thought of them as being so self-sufficient that they'd be insulted if you even asked if they were okay. An older lady in my life would have regarded such any enquiry as being nosey. If you run into that problem, persist, but don't expect much. It took me years to break through her wall of insecurity. She lived a very lonely old age. Don't let that be you. If your interest is spurned, at least you tried and he/she is the loser, and you should love yourself for even trying! You'll find a surprising number of persons do respond gratefully. You'll find that these people become friends for life. It requires letting your own guard down. Have confidence in your ability to be compassionate.

How many people can you think of, who are your own age group, with whom you've never had a real talk? Did they feel free to ask you for help when they had a divorce, a death in the family, a child who was difficult . . . think; what should you have done? Did you miss an opportunity, could you have helped? Then, make the assumption it would have been appreciated, and they may have given you this type of love in return.

Here we need a bit of a warning. Don't be a leaning post to the ones who will take advantage. More than once lately I've been hearing about those types. Perhaps it is part of being older. Listen. Make appropriate suggestions of solutions. If then, they return not having done anything, just give them the same suggestions, the 'solutions" they did not do. "Hang up" literally, if it is not working. I know. I know, that is easier said than done if it is a member of the family. The level of friendship I am talking about requires a lot of trust and love, hopefully it occurs with your partner. The friendship love I'm talking about is not sexual. I'm referring to the love that embraces compassion first, and grows into the LOVE which is the love Jesus talks about. (If sex is included and if you are not abusing the other person; or if you are not breaking personal commitments, you have a very rich and rare friendship.) For most, this LOVE that is God, is just plain old admiring, caring, and enjoying, and looking forward to being with him/her.

Remember the person, who talks a lot, may not be actually saying his/her real message, the one they really wish you to hear. What is said may just be in the eyes. The eyes are the windows of the soul, truthfully. You see pain, or passion, there first. It is a reason I question, "Why are the women who are wearing burqas have only their eyes showing?" Don't the men who insist on hiding their wives faces know the real "come-on expressions" are transmitted by those "hidden" eyes? Girls in bars and on the streets use these techniques! The girls I taught who were "working" in the street used to tease me, and say they could make more money in a night than I did in a month. They said that, not only was I too old to make such cash, but that I wouldn't have the right eye contact. Be bold in your search for those who need your understanding. Ask those pain-filled eyes, if they are feeling alright. Gain a new real friend.

I think that with so many people, one has only to contribute a little of your own thinking about your own experiences, and then one hears maybe more than the speaker even intended. I know that often I try to talk, and am interrupted. I refer to this as talking on the surface. I know some people who talk, but do not really, really talk. I guess they believe it would be a sign of weakness to let anyone know of personal suffering. In this case, try physical touch. There are times when everyone needs a good solid, warm, genuine hug. That just might be the way to break through. Our Anglo Saxon culture does not lend itself easily to physical touches, let alone hugs. Is it because we are so afraid that there might be a sexual contact? What a lot you are missing if this is your idea! When I visit my Muslim friends, I get wonderful hugs. There is so much love in the family that they can't help but share it with everyone they adopt as a friend. They have Jesus as one of their prophets, and they followed His dictum better than we do.

If, when you were "down" and you had a hug from a friend whom you believed really cared about you, wouldn't you feel better? These are the "real" friends who do love you. A hug is just about caring for the other person deeply. If you are lucky, your hugging friends are both male and female. They genuinely like you, and will listen when you expound for a long time about your problems; they do not have to give solutions just willing ears! They let you come to your own conclusions. Their friendship is a "gift" you have earned! I have occasionally experienced this "hug aversion." Both of us lost out.

Many wiser people than I have written volumes about how such sharing friendships happen. The obvious suggestion is that if you want to have a trusted friend, then you must be one. Help where you can see it is needed.

Sometimes you must break down a barrier. The most obvious of such walls are differences in age, monetary status, education, religion, culture, and language. Probably, you can think of differences that I did not even mention. If that happens, then you search for a common ground. It is easier for females because most of us have family issues, especially if there are children.

Breaking down barriers is easier, also, if you are comfortable in yourself. If you are envious, or covetous by nature, your own unhappiness is expressed in your tone of voice and in your body language. If you are a happy person, others know pretty fast. It all comes back to what I've been saying throughout the writing. Love yourself first, only then you can be a loving, happy human. Isn't that the most important thing in life? I heard it said once about people from Newfoundland that they were so personally secure and confident that they could talk to anyone with no sense of inferiority . . . even to the Queen. They did that in spades on royal visits! Apparently, our Queen loves Newfoundlanders too.

Don't hesitate to have a friend of the opposite sex. I find "guys" are great company. It is refreshing to get a totally new perspective on a problem for which I did not know all answers. Gay men especially, make wonderful friends as they only expect honest relationships. Most men also appreciate female input, and they will ask things such as, "What did my wife want, or mean, when she did or said that?" I remember one poor new husband. He was in the "dog house" the first Christmas when he gave his wife a wonderful new set of frying pans which she had said she wanted! He learned! Women do appreciate the man's physical help with things such as lifting, and hugs. Don't hesitate, guys! Girls won't bite, usually.

If there is a problem of not having friends, ask yourself as honestly as you can if your own character problems are standing in your way. Are you approachable, or are you acting shy, superior, judgemental, or annoyed at being spoken to? You must have the appearance of being a person, who wants someone to talk to you, before they will. I'll talk to anyone who smiles at me . . . well almost. I do take a bit of caution if leering is obvious. It is all so much easier now that I'm an older person, and look friendly. I get called "honey" and "dear" frequently. I was given a locker of my own at the health club last month just because I am known as being friendly. Take a chance. Being told to get lost isn't that painful, when you love yourself.

Rule 25

You Must Appreciate God's World

We tend to regard our world, and all that is in it, with awe. There is the common belief that it is our gift from God and exists for our benefit. It is our Garden of Eden, ours because God loves us so much. Like the ancient people of Eurasia, we are encouraged to believe that as long as we are being "good", God will leave us alone to enjoy all that it offers. Those ancient people were very surprised when the Ring of Fire exploded because of the shifting tectonic plates all around them; it is speculated that there may even have been a comet strike in the Pacific Ocean! Did God send this destruction as punishment because they were so evil and had forgotten to worship Him?

These very ancient (30,000-20,000 B.C.) cataclysmic horrors are slowly being discovered and understood by archaeologists, and underwater explorers. It is now accepted as being all part of the natural forces of creation: the changing of the earth's crust, and the movements in the heavenly bodies, such as comets. The surviving original inhabitants fled their inundated homes and lands and went by water to other areas. Their gods and beliefs went with them. There are many signs of the resettlements, which are now being discovered in other Pacific islands and in South and North America. Undoubtedly, they swore to be better people, so their gods would not punish them again.

Recently, however, there are present day happenings of these magnitudes, and our churches are not being better attended. Witness the fall of the Cathedral in New Zealand, and there apparently was no questioning of the expressed need to rebuild. Yet, that church was not well attended, and there has been no great religious revival there. It was the same for most places of worship. Does this mean that we do not notice, nor believe, that the creator, God, who gave us this beautiful world, would not then punish us for disobedience? Personally, I believe, as do many people today, there are always going to be changes in earth's crust, atmosphere and surrounding heavens. To me these are natural happenings, not punishments. What do you think? Is it God's will? Your answer will be based on your belief system.

We can't, however, help but feel awe, not only when disasters occur, but also when we are *out enjoying nature*. I use the word, "awe" not as in the common usage of the word, to mean anything that is positive. By "awe", I mean what the people feel when they are walking in a green and peaceful forest. They feel God's loving presence surrounding them. Consequently, they may say they do not feel any need to actually go into a church to be with God. For me, the ultimate natural experience of God's love comes when I am walking beside the ocean. The waves would be thundering, the air would be fresh, and the gulls would be crying. I hope you have a spot in nature that gives you this "awe", this *God-feeling*.

Perhaps your idea of communing with nature is to have the unconditional love of an animal. There is nothing like coming home from a difficult day at work and being greeted by an enthusiastic dog. He'll be as anxious to go out for a walk as you are, (hopefully). In such circumstances, a cat may even deign to notice your presence. Our neighbour's cat, the beautiful Juliet, comes to get her pats whenever I go out to hang out the laundry. Perhaps you like night walks, and you admire the constant changes in the heavens. I used to walk Angus, our dog, in the night; I miss watching the changes in the night sky.

Perhaps you have discovered that you do not have to be in a forest or beside a brook to get this feeling. It really is here in the city. Make use of our many parks. When we first started the trips to our park, there were muskrats and king fisher birds. They all left our park when the city started to use the creek to drain the effluent from the airport. There is, however, still the lovely rippling sound of the brown water. In contrast to our many parks in Toronto, I've seen the beautiful very private parks in London, England. The key for the gate is available only to the local residents! Ours are free; we are more fortunate.

Perhaps you can feel the same "awe" when you experience such natural connections indirectly. Do you respond to a painting? Do you respond to beautiful poetry? Do you respond to a cardinal's song? Does a certain type of music move you? Recently, I heard of an experiment that proved that mice recovered more quickly from surgery when they listened to Mozart or Verde. I think a lot of older men get a lift just by seeing a beautiful girl walk by. Remember the line of the song, "Beautiful girls, and walk a little slower when you walk by me?"

What is this sense of "awe"? How does it give us such a happy, warm feeling, such a feeling of security? I believe it is a manifestation of God's all-encompassing LOVE. The churches have realized this. For ages, they have made extensive use of beautiful art and music to increase the sensation. Some people only come to church for these bits of inspiration. The atmosphere is set for joyous celebration, or for quiet thought and prayer.

Funeral homes, which are used for secular memorial services, also make use of these same techniques. At secular memorial services, why is it a frequent request to have the ashes scattered in the forest, or on the ocean? Why do these people say that they believe there is a God, reverence His creation, but refuse to be seen in a church, even for their final good bye? Did terrible life experiences lead to different answers? Do they really believe that God is responsible for all the destruction, and the evil in the world?

These questions lead to an inevitable one: How can we say that we understand and appreciate creation, yet we constantly seem to abuse the world? How can we expect this beautiful world with all its awe inspiring forces to be around for our descendants?

The only answer, which makes any sense, is that we must live, not only with the awe, but also with respect in creation. We must be world guardians and sustainers to the best of our abilities. We are not here to change the evolutionary processes. God, or the force of creation, changes the shape of the world, not we. Our children, and their children, and their children's children, and . . . None of them will live in the same physical world we live in. I've been reading about the people who existed long before recorded history. I used to think the Egyptian civilization was old. No, it wasn't! There were advanced civilizations around the Pacific long before the people even lived in Mesopotamia. Think of the huge structures off the coast of Japan which are believed to be thousands of years old. It all makes for great reading. What a lot of history we never learned in school!

Yes I agree, lately, there have been major changes in our weather, and the world is warming. We've recently had what we call a wonderful winter with almost no snow. Did the people in Eastern Europe say the same? I guess not! There have been differences in the sunspots, and in the Northern Lights. Are these things all related? Who Knows? Is the sun a significant influence? This has been a year of earthquakes and volcanic eruptions. Are they the cause of the weather changes? Do scientists know for sure what is happening? No! We all know, however, that one big volcanic eruption can put more carbon ash in the atmosphere than do all the cars on earth with their bits of carbon emission. It is very presumptuous of humans to believe, that the little we do, can influence the world's creative forces. We can merely understand that, and be in awe.

Archaeologists and geologists have ascertained that 10,000 to 12,000 years ago, when the last ice age melted, there were great changes in the landmasses, and that the continents on our globe were and are now continually shifting. The people who escaped these old upheavals fled and held their beliefs. Hence, we read about the sacrificing of young female virgins in the Mayan observances. We tend to regard such ideas as ridiculous, but how then should we live with respect in Creation?

We start by training our children. When a gum wrapper is tossed, the thrower is told to pick it up. He/she is also taught to put it in the garbage. In Canada, the elementary schools now are doing a good job of increasing this awareness. On a larger scale, where do we put that garbage we've trained children to collect? At present, the solution is not wonderful. I believe it could be. We just need to make that a priority for our governments. We could be world leaders here with a little more money, ingenuity, and research. Have you ever been in a third world country? Throughout our planet there is still a lot of teaching to do. Cuba was pretty good because of the scavenging due to poverty. Venezuela was littered almost everywhere we went, especially along the roads.

Our current city council is making an effort to remove graffiti in public areas. There have been some objections as some of the art is actually pretty good. It is still, however, on someone else's property and is not right! This removal idea is based on an idea from Chicago. There was a man who made people aware that one broken window leads to many others, so repairs should be done immediately to avoid more damage. We even saw a programme, which showed that if a house was not sold after a certain number of years, it was torn down. That prevented vandals and drug abusers from moving in. Occasionally, on a highway, one sees a sign that a certain club or an office group has adopted a stretch of the road. This is a small start for the problem of our highway garbage. Obviously, some businesses and large institutions have accepted the idea that they have a responsibility to clean up our world. Our governments are not above using a little pressure here too. Specifically, we know that some Canadian companies needed that pressure to improve their ways in Africa, and other countries where they have operations. Is it too late? Shouldn't we be putting more such pressure on our Members of Parliament?

Another area, where there is hope, is in the field of science. I think we have merely scratched the surface of what we may learn that will help preserve the planet for the coming population explosion. They will *all* need more effective and more available birth control. Even now, we are scratching our heads about how they will find enough food. We also need progress in improved sustainability for forests, water, and oil. Why are we avoiding the very practical solution of growing hemp for products such as rope and paper? It is so much more sensible than using the trees we need for oxygen.

I was horrified to read yesterday in the newspaper that Germany has had to admit that their much applauded use off wind and sun generation of electricity is insufficient for their population. They are building many more coal-fired plants—good news for the Ruhr Valley: bad for the atmosphere! My husband, who is an engineer and a reader of "intellectual" publications, has been telling family and friends for a long time that we will be returning to coal! Scientific developments are the best promise for the rescue of the planet. We should learn not to jump onto the latest band wagon so quickly.

We are doing all we are told to do by the media, but we should read more and think more and make our own conclusions. How else will we learn to live with these inevitable earth changes? What else can we do to alleviate the suffering we see on the TV and around us? We know of the Buddhist idea that suffering will always be with us; we know that Jesus also acknowledged suffering. Yet, we must face these realities, and accept our individual responsibility to try to help. You know your own gifts. Use them. Are you a singer like John Denver who taught us to make us even more aware of the beauty around us? Are you able to help in Doctors without Borders? Are you able to build a company to provide jobs for suffering and hungry families? Do your thing. Use your LOVE!

You Must Contribute to the World during Your Life

For many people, this is a novel idea. Why would a person think he/she should improve this world and the lives of those in it? Do you have a goal for your life? Many see the accumulation of money and fame as being their most important goal in life. Others may believe that devoting their lives to "good" causes is the only way to go. Still others believe that a life of worship and mediation is what is *good*. Our father thought that each human being should leave this world a better place than he/she found it. Another group of people will probably think their life's purpose is a question for their future; "I'll deal with it later, when I'm as old as this writer is!" Remember, you may not live as long as I have!

At present, I'm seventy-seven. That is old! I really never think of my age until I have to move around and my husband says, "Be careful now." Friends are saying. "Where is your cane?" So, yes I am a ripe old age. I like to believe that during my life I have done at least one thing that is significant. Have I? Maybe the people I have loved, and those who will read what I'm writing here may be saved from making the errors in judgement which I have made; then, I have made my contribution.

At a young age, I did not consider this question so important. Oh, like most idealistic teenagers I was going to save the world with some great project. That, of course, was after I had an education and had enjoyed my life at college! Then, of course, I had to get married and have a family. Then, of course, I had to be sure that my daughter was launched. Then, of course, I had to teach until I received my pension. Then, of course, I had a retired husband to enjoy, and we had to see as much of the world as possible, before we were too old; we might not be able to do that later! Now, I wonder where the years went.

One way I know that my husband and I both helped was when we could give blood. Also, we never missed a chance to vote. If we were going to be away, we went to the advanced polls. Was it enough to claim that we have done our civic duty, and we contributed to the democracy we have enjoyed? No! Travelling made us well aware of the advantages we have in Canada. Oh, I know we all complain about what the government is doing. Do most of us do anything significant? No. We are fortunate in Canada if we get over a 55% voter turnout. That is disgraceful. We do go to the meetings before elections . . . if we are home. A couple of times we hand delivered literature for a man we hoped would be elected. Have we done enough? No!

In addition, I got a bit of an ego boost lately. A lady, who has taken over the education programme at 'my" jail detention centre, told me that I am fondly remembered there by some of the inmates. She has continued GED education successfully with an enrolment of 12. (There are over 600 inmates doing almost no form of rehabilitation.) She did not get government money for her programme. It is now community sponsored, and she has had to work hard to get that financing. I think she's wonderful, and that is certainly her life's contribution. She produced something useful from nothing. There was also a boost when a former regular school student phoned to tell me that since I'd been there for him through difficulties, and he realized that as I was older, he'd like to be contacted should I ever need help. Did I help other students . . . maybe? I do feel I should have done more. I know of so many other teachers who were so much more giving than I ever was.

I continue to make the odd volunteer contributions of my time through church projects. Is that enough? I am not alone in this 'wondering." Some of my friends "wonder" about their value as volunteers too. The value of our past contributions is a common concern as we are seeing our lives coming to the end. The saddest of all are the friends who now realize that they basically lived only for themselves. They try to justify their lives with meaningless rhetoric. This is why I've tackled this topic. Don't let this be you.

My father and I had this discussion before he died. He told me he thought that his most important accomplishment was that he raised four productive, taxpaying citizens. This was from a man who really did make a huge contribution to secondary education in rural New Brunswick. He was the opening principal for two regional high schools in New Brunswick. This was after the war. Before 1947, students only received a leaving certificate at the end of Grade 10. It did not allow one to attend a university. He was so busy with his schools that my mother should have also counted us as her contribution! He found his later work with Indian Affairs very discouraging, yet I'm sure he did help some people.

Even sadder was Mary, of whom I've spoken earlier. She had spent her life always doing what was expected, and following the idea that she "had" to be a helper to all. Don't let that happen either. She did help me to understand that when you help others, it should be what you want to do, rather than what you feel you should do. That is the better way. You get your own "lift", instead of it having been done with resentment. There were times when I couldn't have done my job without her help around my house. She told me she was happy being with us. She had learned this was what God intended when Jesus told us to love others as much as we love ourselves. At first, when I met Mary there was still a problem with the self-love. To many people, even those who go to church "religiously", these instructions prove to be a dilemma. So, what is the answer? I will try to answer by giving examples of some of the people I believe who have found a path to self-love as well as a good attitude for helping others. Maybe at least one of these examples will help you to understand.

I already mentioned there were many teachers who gave willingly to their students, more than I ever did. I'll tell you about Miss Wilson. I met her just after she retired. Fifty years ago, we had moved into a new apartment building in Weston. She lived across the hall and welcomed us. The next day, she explained the amenities of the building, the history of the "village" and why she was so happy to live there.

Miss Wilson had gone to Northern Ontario to teach after graduation from Normal School. It was in a country school, and she'd liked it and was successful. After a couple of years she had to make a decision. There was a marriage proposal. She could have left teaching, raised a family and lived there for the rest of her life. Married women could not teach in those days. Her decision, instead, was to get a job in Toronto, and go to university to upgrade her qualifications. Her life was spent teaching at Western Collegiate. She had taken enough extra courses and became recognized as Head of Home Economics.

She was never one to brag; I had to glean from the stories I heard from her, and from former students that her contribution to their lives was great. She loved her students, and in many cases replaced the parents they never had. Marriage was not in the cards as the year she came to Toronto was 1919. Too many of the men her age had died in the war, and in the ensuing flu epidemic.

Now, did she love herself? You bet. I have always modelled myself on her for grooming, but more importantly, her sense of style. She was never out of date. Even, in her old age, she insisted on having the best mink coat. She inspired me to insist that my husband and I travel whenever we could. She would insist on looking after our mail and our apartment. Miss Coburn always travelled alone. That way, she said, she met more interesting people. She had been to England many times and had known it well. Hence, our first big trip was to see all the Cathedrals about which she had given us her guide books. Her regular attendance at her church and the large bequest at her death left no doubt that following Jesus" commandment was a guide to her Life.

Maybe, in your life, the way you are contributing is to add beauty to the world. I think particularly of the value of "good" music. What that means is very individual. Whatever you find relaxing, or exhilarating, is good to you. Your favourite musicians and composers really have made a contribution to your life. Are you one of these musicians? It has been shown lately that such a response to your sound is very beneficial for people who have serious psychological problems, such as Post Traumatic Stress Syndrome.

Maybe your idea of beauty is artwork. Are you a painter like one of my best friends? Her home is like an art gallery! I have copies of many other paintings which have moved me: some to tears! When I go to bed and wake up I look at a copy of a picture of two little girls by Paul Kane. It is titled "After the Bath." The first time I saw it at the AGO, I was so moved that I burst into tears. I love and have copies of the group of seven for instance. One of my close friends has these copies too, and they speak to him also. He is an avid orienteer and is most at home in the forests.

Do you sing? Do you paint? If you do not, do you add beauty to the world by just refusing to be a slob? My husband certainly gets a lot of joy from admiring young healthy ladies who have happy faces; especially if they are friendly! He maintains that the most attractive thing about a woman of any age is her smile. I catch him looking, and talking to all friendly ladies. This type of "looking" also, of course, applies to us "girl's, but did we never, ever let men know? We would not have even dared to be so "forward"! Young women are now learning to acknowledge their interest in attractive men, and are enjoying life and having more fun than we ever did. Do you realize that "ladies" in our generation never dared to be obviously appreciative of a good male physique? Our loss!

So, contributing to the world means helping people, and being kind to them at the same time. Remember, "friendliness" is a big way of helping; it requires so little effort. The rewards are enormous. Do you notice the nametag on the front the clerk's shirt when you are in a store? Do you use the name and say, "Thank you, "name." ? The smile you'll get can set your good mood for the day. I'll bet that happens rarely. Why don't people make these small gestures? I believe it is thoughtlessness in most cases. Perhaps, any reticence is based on the old thinking that the person will find you "too forward." Perhaps you were raised with the rule that one cannot talk to strangers. What a horror we have created with that idea! Once when my grandson was young, he questioned me after I talked to a lady who was lonely looking. She had responded well. Afterward, he said, "Did you know her, Baba?" Sad . . . You bet!

I can't leave this topic without a comment for those in the helping professions. I'll refer first to the teachers. I've been retired so long that I'll tell of what I learn from those who are presently teaching from my family. They keep me informed about the existing work conditions. There is regularly a new government paper to explain the "new" ideas of how they should teach their subjects. These edicts demand many training sessions after school, and much study of the work of the "experts." This is for people who have already decided what is applicable for their students in their particular environment! The teachers are feeling a great deal of time stress, as well as doubt about the usefulness of the new ideas. I recall when I was told that teaching grammar was forbidden. Based on the writing my students were doing, I realized that was wrong. I occasionally would close the door and tell the class that I was about to commit an illegal act. They loved it. Then I'd do something such as use the verb "to love", and we'd discuss the use of the past tenses. We had fun; it is not illegal!

In some schools now the discipline is difficult, or nonexistent, all due to lack of office support. Students are too quick to assert their "rights" if they are disciplined. If that doesn't get action they call a parent who calls a lawyer or the press. Hence, no matter what the offense the principal is in trouble, and consequently rendered ineffectual. I retired in time! One of my relatives recently had to hire her own lawyer when a member of a gang threatened her physically.

I also have young friends in the health care professions. The stress levels there are high also. Again, the government's ideas of improving the care are not often based of the reality of what actions are required. These people (particularly nurses) tell me that they wish they'd be seriously consulted before being told that this is "the new way things will be done." Students who have university degrees in nursing are required to work for six months under a nurse who has a college R.N. because their practicum is insufficient. Guess who receives the higher salary . . . right!

Perhaps the saddest of all are the people who are staying in the helping professions, but still say they believe they are not fulfilling their lives" purposes; that they should have done more. Where does that guilt and self-punishment come from? I think of the professional engineer who had a good career, and helped to make our roads safe. He was told by his mother that he should have done more. Did he do what he could? Did he contribute? Yes!

I've left to the end the people who are in business, and are often abused as being those who put self-interest first. (Think of the 1% rallies.) Yes, many do well financially, but consider this: where would ninety-per cent of the population get work, if there were no businesses to provide jobs? Remember what I told you about the enormous help my husband's father was to his community. Did he even get rich? No! My husband was one of those "terrible people" called an "investment banker." I lost count of how many companies he helped to establish. Other family members are business professors and some are consultants. Think how large their contributions will be to the world of work. They are where they should be, and they should be allowed to feel good about themselves and appreciate their rewards if they are lucky enough to receive them. They are making their large contributions to the world of work!

When he was older, Frank Sinatra's most popular song, both for himself and for many of his audiences was, "I Did It My Way" He certainly had a "chequered" past; yet he sounded content with the life he'd led and with his contribution. Will you be? Did you use your God given free will, and your wisdom to decide on what your contribution to your world would be? Did you do it just to please others and your God? Did you do it all because you truly felt no resentment; was it just your need to express LOVE? If so you'll be likely to have a peaceful journey at your death

Conclusion

Do You Still Have an Invisible Burqa?

I n other words, do you still follow all the rules you've just read about? Are you planning to forget that I asked you to consider alternative answers to life's questions? Are you staying with all the ideas that you were introduced to as a child, or as a young person? They will definitely make your life more comfortable in the short term. It will certainly keep your old parents, your minister, your priest, or your spiritual leader happier. They will continue in their beliefs that they have lead you on the right path, and that you will never suffer pangs of conscience, nor will you go to hell when you eventually die. As long as you don't think about what you are doing, or ever question any of these ideas. You can also probably live without much guilt. Will you have fulfilled your potential? Will you know in yourself that you have done the things Jesus, or any other of the religious prophets, suggested? Will you have fulfilled your potential? Will you have contributed all you could to your world?

Have you started to think about the consequences of following these old rules? There was an article in the National Post, June 4, 2012. It was about the intense questioning that young educated people in their twenties and thirties are struggling with *now*. How can one contribute to the world now and still have enough money to survive? Can you have both? I did. Was it hard work, or luck? (Probably it was more luck!) If you are young, career choices should be made only by you; just be sure to check with all sources of information before you decide. Remember many people have had several jobs in their lifetimes. My husband was educated for three different jobs and did all three at different times.

A New York Times article by David Brooks claims many young people, especially graduates trained for the professions, are questioning life choices. They do not even have the background in religion or philosophy, or a vocabulary to discuss what their choices are. There has been no discussion in their lives of any religion, or of any value system. The parents often were too busy. They rely almost entirely on the information and values expressed in the many forms of the media to which they are exposed. They are probably convinced that they want to be "good guys" like Bono, but they don't understand how. Or, perhaps they have seen how really well the really rich live, and have decided that they want a slice of that pie! Just try to do the latter in today's economic climate unless you inherit a lot of cash!

If you are one of these questioning young people, give some thought to the ideas which I have been expressing. My friend, Mary, died in peace, knowing that she had done as Jesus told us God wanted her to do. She acknowledged the powerful force of love, which is God, she helped others, and she learned to love herself. I believe when I die I will have the same peace. Will You? Why, or why not?

I repeat, I am not advocating any church, or any certain organized religion just because I have found it helpful. There can be too much serious persuasive talk which tends to drive people away from any belief in the LOVE of God. I know our New Testament tells us that Jesus would like us to let everyone know about God's LOVE. That is what I am doing with this writing. I have faith that it will reach, and be a help to some people . . . maybe not in my lifetime. I will know, however, that I have tried. God's love can't be forced by fear; only by practicing it can we learn to love as He wishes us to.

Here are some ideas which might help you to the realization that my beliefs are worth considering. Most of us have recently had to consider the idea of the enormous IT cloud to which all our media communications have ascended. It was not a great stretch of imagination to do so. Now, think of the power of God's LOVE as such a huge cloud, which is surrounding our world. (No, there is not a nasty old, bearded, judgemental man up there.) Remember as I said earlier, there are many religions which advocate only these three ideas I have stressed as a basis for living life. They see God as a LOVE force, a force that it is multiplied by human goodness. They all have different prophets and wise men, but the basics are identical. I'm going to quote from a novel I have just read about life in Afghanistan.

This book was written by Deborah Rodriguez and is titled, "The Little Coffee Shop of Kabul." At the end of the story, a very strictly religious young Muslim man falls in love. Formerly, he had wanted to kill people of other faiths. Love changed him: "It turned a serious boy into a generous man. This is the real Islam, the Islam of love, not hate. Muhammad would be proud, he thought." (Page 270) My friends who are practising Muslims believe the same.

Yes, we may have grown up with different ways of showing God that we acknowledge his LOVE. I am sure that He understands why we are all different in our expressions and practices. First, can you honestly say that you love yourself. This requires serious soul searching and sometimes help. As you have read here, once there is self-love, then you can look at others with compassion and be some honest help to them. Again, look in those eyes, the windows of the soul. I could see this type of intense feeling of need in a picture of the crowd at Eaton Centre recently. It showed the horror and fear in the eyes of those who had witnessed that dreadful shooting. It is a most unusual person who does not indicate suffering in the eyes. As I said before, the help you offer may be the only kindness they've ever experienced, for a long time, or even in their lives. Yours is a start. When you see pain or need, just talk and then listen. All that they can do is to be rude, and say, "Get lost!" That tells you how great the need was. Only loving compassion generates all types of love, and leads you to understand and experience the Love of God.

It may take a while, but I believe that you will realize that you are seeing the world as a better place, and you are feeling happier. Is this the power of God's love working through you? Yes.